MYSTAGOGY

MYSTAGOGY

Liturgical Paschal Spirituality
for Lent and Easter

Mark G. Boyer

ALBA · HOUSE   NEW · YORK

SOCIETY OF ST. PAUL, 2187 VICTORY BLVD., STATEN ISLAND, NEW YORK 10314

Library of Congress Cataloging-in-Publication Data

Boyer, Mark G.
    Mystagogy: liturgical paschal spirituality for Lent and Easter /
Mark G. Boyer.
       p.   cm.
    ISBN 0-8189-0563-8
    1. Lent — Prayer-books and devotions — English. 2. Eastertide —
Prayer-books and devotions — English.   3. Spiritual exercises.
I. Title.
BX2170.L4B69   1990   89-28614
242'.34 — dc20   CIP

Designed, printed and bound in the United States of
America by the Fathers and Brothers of the
Society of St. Paul, 2187 Victory Boulevard,
Staten Island, New York 10314, as part of their
communications apostolate.

Printing Information:

Current Printing - first digit   1   2   3   4   5   6   7   8   9   10   11   12

Year of Current Printing - first year shown
1990   1991   1992   1993   1994   1995   1996   1997

DEDICATED TO

The Most Reverend J. Leibrecht,
a shepherd who continues to grow with the sheep
in living and celebrating the paschal mystery.

ABBREVIATIONS

DB   *Dictionary of the Bible*. John L. McKenzie. Milwaukee:
     The Bruce Publishing Company, 1965.
DCA "Dedication of a Church and an Altar." *The Rites*.
     Volume Two. New York: Pueblo Publishing
     Company, 1980.
EV   "The Easter Vigil." *The Sacramentary*. New York:
     Catholic Book Publishing Company, 1985.
GF   "Good Friday." *The Sacramentary*. New York:
     Catholic Book Publishing Company, 1985.
LH   *The Liturgy of the Hours*. Volume II: Lenten Season,
     Easter Season. New York: Catholic Book Publishing
     Company, 1970.
NDT *The New Dictionary of Theology*. Joseph A.
     Komonchak, Mary Collins, Dermot A. Lane, eds.
     Wilmington, Delaware: Michael Glazier, Inc., 1987.
PCPF "Preparing and Celebrating the Paschal Feasts."
     Circular Letter of the Congregation for Divine
     Worship, January 16, 1988. *Origins*. Vol. 17: No. 40;
     March 17, 1988.
RBC "Rite of Baptism for Children." *The Rites*. Volume
     One. New York: Pueblo Publishing Company, 1976.
RCIA *Rite of Christian Initiation of Adults*. Washington, DC:
     United States Catholic Conference, 1988.
TS   *The Sacramentary*. New York: Catholic Book
     Publishing Company, 1985.

"The arrangement of the names of Christ . . . is manifold: LORD, because He is Spirit; WORD, because He is God; SON, because He is the only-begotten Son of the Father; MAN, because He was born of the Virgin; PRIEST, because He offered Himself as a sacrifice; SHEPHERD, because He is a guardian; WORM, because He rose again; MOUN-TAIN, because He is strong; WAY, because there is a straight path through Him to life; LAMB, because He suffered; CORNER-STONE, because instruction is His; TEACHER, because He demonstrates how to live; SUN, because He is the illuminator; TRUTH, because He is from the Father; LIFE, because He is the creator; BREAD, because He is flesh; SAMARITAN, because He is the merciful protector; CHRIST, because He is anointed; JESUS, because He is the Savior; GOD, because He is of God; AN-GEL, because He was sent; BRIDEGROOM, because He is a mediator; VINE, because we are redeemed by His blood; LION, because He is king; ROCK, because He is firm; FLOWER, because He is the chosen one; PROPHET, because He has revealed what is to come."

The Decree of Damasus, 382 AD
St. Damasus I, Pope 366-384 AD

TABLE OF CONTENTS

INTRODUCTION

When the Constitution on the Liturgy of Vatican Council II declared that "all the faithful should be led to that full, conscious, and active participation in liturgical celebrations which is demanded by the very nature of the liturgy, and to which the Christian people . . . have a right and obligation by reason of their baptism" (#14), the Church also realized that education was an important and necessary tool to accomplish this norm. This book aims at contributing to the education and formation of people in the liturgical paschal spirituality of the Church during Lent and Easter.

It is titled *Mystagogy*, which means catechesis or ongoing formation. For the person who was baptized, confirmed, and received eucharist for the first time at the Easter Vigil, the fifty days from Easter Sunday to Pentecost Sunday is his or her "period of postbaptismal catechesis or mystagogy, marked by the new experience of sacraments and community." (RCIA #7)

"This is a time for the community and the neophytes together to grow in deepening their grasp of the paschal mystery and in making it part of their lives through meditation on the Gospel, sharing in the eucharist, and doing the works of charity." (RCIA #244)

The newly baptized, or neophytes, are "introduced into a fuller and more effective understanding of mysteries through the Gospel message they have learned and above all through their experience of the sacraments they have received. For they have truly been renewed in mind, tasted more deeply the sweetness of God's word, received the fellowship of the Holy Spirit, and grown to know the goodness of the Lord. Out of this experience, which belongs to Christians and increases as it is lived, they derive a new perception of the faith, of the Church, and of the world." (RCIA #245)

The ongoing formation of the newly baptized is not meant to leave out those who have been the Church for many years. These persons must also continue their growth in understanding of the paschal mystery. These, too, must continue to come to a new perception of the faith, of the Church, and of the world.

This is urged in the Circular Letter from the Congregation for Divine Worship entitled "Preparing and Celebrating the Paschal Feasts," dated January 16, 1988, and released February 20, 1988. "For a better celebration of the Easter Vigil," the letter states, "it is necessary that pastors themselves have an ever deeper knowledge of both text and rites so as to give a proper mystagogical catechesis to the people." (PCPF #96)

Such a mystagogical catechesis is what this book attempts to give. The fifty-four exercises are divided according to eight themes: (1) on this most holy night, (2) Christ has ransomed us with his blood, (3) this passover mystery, (4) A flame divided but undimmed, (5) washed clean of sin, (6) how boundless your merciful love, (7) perfection, and (8) go!

Each exercise consists of a quotation from the liturgy of the Church or the Scriptures used in the liturgy during the Easter Triduum, a catechetical reflection/instruction, questions for personal meditation, and a prayer taken from the sourcebook of the Church's collection of prayers, *The Sacramentary*.

This book is subtitled "Liturgical Paschal Spirituality for Lent and Easter." Liturgy is the work of the people, the community called Church. The Constitution on the Liturgy declares that the liturgy is "the summit toward which the activity of the Church is directed [and] the fount from which all her power flows." (#10) The use of materials from *The Sacramentary* makes each exercise one that flows directly from the liturgical wealth of the Church.

This is a book about the paschal mystery — the passover of Jesus from death to life and the ongoing passover of Christians from death to life. The core sections of the book, "this passover mystery," "a flame divided but undimmed," and "washed clean of sin," deal with the suffering, death, resurrection, ascension, and gift of the Spirit from Jesus as well as with each Christian's suffering, dying, new life, new vision, and experience of the fire of the Spirit in the midst of the Christian community.

Spirituality pervades the entire book from the opening quotation of each exercise to the concluding prayer of each reflection. Through the questions provided for personal meditation, a person may permit God to breathe into him or her. This mingling of the breath of God and the breath of people is spirituality; this is how one knows what God's will is and, then, is able to do it.

Chapter Nine consists of eight group exercises which roughly correspond to the eight themes mentioned above. Each group exercise is composed of a lengthy quotation from one of the early Fathers of the Church, five questions for group discussion, and a prayer to conclude the period of discussion. The exercises in this chapter can be used during gatherings of catechumens during the Lenten Season or gatherings of neophytes during the Easter Season. It is recommended that the exercise be read and answers prepared for the questions by each member of the group before all gather together.

This book can be used during Lent, during Easter, or during both of these liturgical seasons. Both those persons preparing during Lent for the Easter Sacraments (Baptism, Confirmation, Eucharist) at the Easter Vigil and those who are already baptized and spend Lent preparing for the Easter Triduum by reflecting on their baptism will find this book to be an aid in their formation. Conversion continues after the celebration of the Easter Sacraments for everyone. By immersing oneself into the paschal mystery and reflecting on the liturgical paschal spirituality of the Church, a person is gradually incorporated and re-incorporated into the stream of the new life of the Church.

If this book is used during the forty days of Lent, it can be continued during the first two weeks of Easter. Otherwise, it may be started on Wednesday of Holy Week and used throughout the fifty days of the Easter Season to Pentecost Sunday. It might also be started during the middle of Lent and used until the middle of Easter. If begun on Ash Wednesday, by spending more than one day on an exercise, a person could use the book throughout the Lenten and Easter Seasons.

Through instruction, meditation, and prayer, a model is provided for the Season of Ordinary Time which follows the Easter Season. Both the clergy and the laity will find a wealth of mystagogy in the pages which follow. It is hoped that through catechesis and prayer the Church will be continually built up and grow into the likeness of Christ through the paschal mystery.

Mark G. Boyer

MYSTAGOGY

Chapter One

ON THIS MOST HOLY NIGHT

1. *"The Church invites her children throughout the world/ to come together in vigil and prayer."* (EV #8)

The peak of the liturgical year is the Easter Triduum — Holy Thursday-Good Friday, Good Friday-Holy Saturday, and Holy Saturday-Easter Sunday. The liturgy of Holy Thursday commemorates "the institution of the eucharist, the institution of the priesthood, and Christ's commandment of love" (TS, p. 136) as exemplified in the washing of the feet ceremony. On Good Friday the universal Church celebrates the Lord's passion and death. Then, during Holy Saturday night "people keep prayerful vigil." (EV #45) The Easter Vigil of Holy Saturday unites the themes of Holy Thursday and Good Friday in one grand celebration of new life.

The invitation issued to all people by the Church is to gather together in vigil and prayer. The vigil motif finds its origin in the Hebrew Scriptures' Book of Exodus. The escape of the Israelites from the Egyptians took place during the night. *This was a night of vigil for the Lord, as he led them out of the land of Egypt; so on this same night all the Israelites must keep a vigil for the Lord throughout their generations.* (Exodus 12:42) Also, for Christians, "this night is one of vigil for the Lord." (EV #1)

The Easter Vigil commemorates "that holy night when the Lord rose from the dead." (PCPF #77) It "is regarded as the 'mother of all holy vigils.' For in that night the church keeps vigil, waiting for the resurrection of the Lord." (PCPF #77)

"The entire celebration of the Easter Vigil takes place at night. It should not begin before nightfall; it should end before daybreak on Sunday." (EV #3) "The Passover vigil, in which the Hebrews keep watch for the Lord's Passover, which was to free them from slavery to pharaoh, is an annual commemoration. It prefigured the true Pasch of Christ that was to come, the night that is of true liberation, in which 'destroying the bonds of death, Christ rose as victor from the depths.' " (PCPF # 79)

The Easter Vigil, then, "is the solemnity of solemnities. . . . The full meaning of the vigil is a waiting for the coming of the Lord." (PCPF #80).

The second motif of the Easter Vigil is prayer. During the night watch of the resurrection of the Lord Jesus Christ, people come together to pray "by hearing his word and celebrating his mysteries." (EV #8) Through the liturgy of the word, "the Church meditates on all the wonderful things God has done for his people from the beginning." (EV #2) This is accomplished by means of nine readings, "seven from the Old Testament and two from the New Testament (the epistle and gospel)." (EV #20)

In celebrating the mysteries of the Lord, the Church is not interested in that which is beyond understanding. Rather, mystery is understood as the revelation of God. From the beginning of time God has been revealing himself. Throughout the Easter Vigil, in its signs and words, the Church remembers and celebrates God's gracious uncovering of himself.

The combination of vigil and prayer forms the heart of

the Easter Vigil while at the same time uniting the liturgical themes found in the Holy Thursday and Good Friday celebrations. Vigil and prayer become the "evening sacrifice of praise" (EV #18) of the Church. In the Easter Proclamation (Exsultet), the deacon sings, "Heavenly Father in the joy of this night, receive our evening sacrifice of praise, your Church's solemn offering." (EV #18).

For Reflection

a. When did you last have an experience of waiting (vigiling) for the Lord to come?
b. When did you last hear the word of the Lord? What do you remember that you heard?
c. In what way has God most recently revealed himself to you?

Prayer

God our Father,/every year we rejoice/as we look forward to this feast of our salvation./May we welcome Christ as our Redeemer,/and meet him with confidence when he comes to be our judge,/who lives and reigns with you and the Holy Spirit,/one God, for ever and ever. Amen. (TS, p. 38)

2. *"This is the night when Jesus Christ/broke the chains of death and rose triumphant from the grave."* (EV #18)

For three days Jesus was held prisoner by death. Just as bars confine a criminal in a prison, so the grave functioned as Jesus' maximum security cell. However, on this "most blessed of all nights, chosen by God to see Christ rising from

the dead" (EV #18), there are no witnesses to Jesus' escape
— other than God and the darkness itself.

The night of the greatest prisoner escape in history is
set aside as holy; it is sacred; it is set apart. How ironic that
the darkness observed the great event of light! In all four
gospel accounts of the resurrection of Jesus, the event has
already taken place by the time that the women arrive at the
tomb.

After the sabbath, as the first day of the week was dawning,
Mary Magdalene and the other Mary came to see the tomb. . . . An
angel of the Lord descended from heaven, approached, rolled back
the stone, and sat upon it. Then the angel said to the women . . . , "Do
not be afraid! I know that you are seeking Jesus the crucified. He is
not here, for he has been raised just as he said. Come and see the place
where he lay." (Matthew 28:1-2, 5-6)

When the sabbath was over, Mary Magdalene, Mary, the
mother of James, and Salome bought spices that they might go and
anoint him. Very early when the sun had risen, on the first day of the
week, they came to the tomb. They were saying to one another, "Who
will roll back the stone for us from the entrance to the tomb?" When
they looked up, they saw that the stone had been rolled back; it was
very large. On entering the tomb they saw a young man sitting on the
right side, clothed in a white robe, and they were utterly amazed. He
said to them, "Do not be amazed! You seek Jesus of Nazareth, the
crucified. He has been raised; he is not here. Behold, the place where
they laid him." (Mark 16:1-6)

But at daybreak on the first day of the week they took the spices
they had prepared and went to the tomb. They found the stone rolled
away from the tomb; but when they entered, they did not find the body
of the Lord Jesus. While they were puzzling over this, behold, two
men in dazzling garments appeared to them. They were terrified and
bowed their faces to the ground. They said to them, "Why do you seek
the living one among the dead? He is not here, but he has been
raised." (Luke 24:1-6)

On the first day of the week, Mary of Magdala came to the tomb early in the morning, while it was still dark, and saw the stone removed from the tomb. So she ran and went to Simon Peter and to the other disciple whom Jesus loved, and told them, "They have taken the Lord from the tomb, and we don't know where they put him." So Peter and the other disciple went out and came to the tomb. . . . Simon Peter . . . went into the tomb and saw the burial cloths there. . . . Then the other disciple also went in, . . . and he saw and believed. (John 20:1-3, 6, 8)

It is important to realize that the resurrection is not resuscitation, a bringing back to life of a seemingly-dead body. A person who is resuscitated will still die some day. One who has been raised has passed through death to deathlessness. Because authentic resurrection is beyond human experience as it is known in its earthly life, there is no adequate way of describing it. All that is available is metaphor — a feeble attempt to capture a reality that is beyond earthly human existence by comparing it to something else. The writers of the gospels employ the empty tomb as a metaphorical attempt to capture the reality of the resurrection of Jesus.

In the liturgy of the Easter Vigil, the Church can do nothing other than exhort rejoicing using the metaphor of light. "Rejoice, O earth, in shining splendor, radiant in the brightness of your King! Rejoice, O Mother Church! Exult in glory! The risen Savior shines upon you!" (EV #18)

The light of the resurrection scatters the darkness of the night of death, just as the writers of the gospel portray the discovery of the empty tomb as taking place at dawn, at sunrise, or early in the morning. The Church picks up this theme as she prays, "Lord God, you have brightened this night with the radiance of the risen Christ." (EV #32)

For Reflection

a. What metaphor do you most frequently use to describe death?
b. What metaphor do you most frequently use to describe resurrection?

Prayer

Father,/you make this holy night radiant/with the splendor of Jesus Christ our light./We welcome him as Lord, the true light of the world./Bring us to eternal joy in the kingdom of heaven, where he lives and reigns with you and the Holy Spirit,/one God, for ever and ever. Amen. (TS, p. 40)

3. *"Of this night scripture says:/'The night will be clear as day:/it will become my light, my joy.'"* (EV #18)

The night of vigil and prayer, during which the resurrection of Jesus is celebrated, is declared to be a day. The resurrection creates greater light than a nuclear flash. The dark night is transformed into joyous day by the sevenfold "power of this holy night." (EV #18)

The Easter Proclamation declares that the brightness of the light of the resurrection (1) dispels all evil, (2) washes guilt away, and (3) restores lost innocence. All three of these themes converge in the liturgy of baptism during which each catechumen renounces evil, is washed in the Spirit-filled waters, and becomes a new creation.

The power of the night (4) brings mourners joy. Not only those who mourned the death of Jesus and brought oils and spices to anoint his body, but those who have mourned the death of anyone find joy in the hope that the resurrection bestows to all people.

Reconciliation is accomplished by this night, which (5) casts out hatred and (6) brings us peace. Resurrection joins God and people together in a union that can only be spoken of as a marriage. "Night truly blessed when heaven is wedded to earth and man [and woman] is reconciled with God," (EV #18) sings the deacon in the Easter Proclamation.

Finally, this holy night has the power to (7) humble earthly pride. People come to realize that they cannot save themselves by their own strength. In fact, strength gets in the way of God's power. God chooses to save people in their human weakness. It was in the human weakness, the suffering, and the death of the human Jesus that God revealed resurrection. "Father, we see your infinite power in your loving plan of salvation. You came to our rescue by your power as God, but you wanted us to be saved by one like us. Man [and woman] refused your friendship, but man himself was to restore it through Jesus Christ our Lord." (TS, p. 435)

It was not in power and might that God saved people; it was in the incarnation and death of his own Son, Jesus. It is in human weakness, in human suffering, and in human death that all touch the depths of humanity. Such human vulnerability is the locus of salvation.

And so the deacon sings, "Jesus Christ, our King, is risen! Christ has conquered! Glory fills you!" (EV #18) Through Christ God has raised up human weakness. He has filled all of human life — especially its weakest moments — with his own glory, his life, his grace, his power. For this great act, the whole universe is exhorted to shout in joy: "Rejoice, heavenly powers! Sing, choirs of angels! Exult, all creation around God's throne." (EV #18)

For Reflection

a. What do you think are the characteristics of human power? of human weakness?
b. What do you think are the characteristics of divine power? of divine weakness?
c. In what ways do you think that people share in God's power?

Prayer

God our Father,/may we look forward with hope to our resurrection,/for you have made us your sons and daughters,/and restored the joy of our youth./We ask this through our Lord Jesus Christ, your Son,/who lives and reigns with you and the Holy Spirit,/one God, for ever and ever. Amen. (TS, p. 226)

Chapter Two

CHRIST HAS RANSOMED US
WITH HIS BLOOD

1. *"Christ has ransomed us with his blood, and paid for us
    the price of Adam's sin . . ."* (EV #18)

The Easter Proclamation declares that people have
been ransomed by Christ. A ransom is a price that is paid. It
is an exchange that is made — one thing for another thing.
In this case, Christ paid his own blood in exchange for the
cancellation of Adam's [and Eve's] sin, which is attributed
with the beginning of death. Life is ransomed by death. "To
ransom a slave you [God] gave away your Son" (EV #18),
sings the deacon. The price of death is paid by death. "O
happy fault, O necessary sin of Adam, which gained for us
so great a Redeemer." (EV #18) Without sin, and ensuing
death, there would have been no need for One to pay the
price of the ransom.

For Reflection

a. In what ways has your life ever been ransomed?
b. How do you think that sin can be considered a happy
    fault?

Prayer

Jesus our Lord,/save us from our sins./Come, protect us from all dangers/and lead us to salvation,/for you live and reign with the Father and the Holy Spirit,/one God, for ever and ever. Amen. (TS, p. 8)

2.   *"What good would life have been to us,/had Christ not come as our Redeemer?"* (EV #18)

Does anyone dare answer this question? The answer is, of course, implied in the question. Life would have had no value in the wake of the first sin and its wave of death. It is the death of Christ which made life valuable. Such irony leaves people with a bittersweet taste. Life is made valuable by death; in fact, death restores life. "Death is the just reward for our sins, yet, when at last we die, your [the Father's] loving kindness calls us back to life in company with Christ, whose victory is our redemption." (TS, p. 535) For "faithful people life is changed, not ended." (TS, p. 527) Therefore, death is not to be feared. Life has been redeemed!

To redeem means, literally, to buy back. Redemption is the "payment of a sum for the release of a person or an object which is held in detention." (DB, p. 723) "The term 'redemption' is best understood as a liberation from one state to another: from bondage to liberation. Redemption is the act or process by which the change takes place." (NDT, p. 837) Life was imprisoned by death; Christ set life free by dying and being raised from the dead by God.

For Reflection

a. Do you fear death? Why?
b. How are you daily engaged in the process of redemption?

Prayer

God our Father,/every year we rejoice/as we look forward to this feast of our salvation./May we welcome Christ as our Redeemer,/and meet him with confidence when he comes to be our judge,/who lives and reigns with you and the Holy Spirit,/one God, for ever and ever. Amen. (TS, p. 38)

3. *"Let us . . . listen attentively to the word of God,/recalling how he saved his people throughout history/and, in the fullness of time,/sent his own Son to be our Redeemer."* (EV #22)

The assembly is invited to listen attentively to the word of God. This means that those present hear and are stirred to their depths by the great events of salvation history. Throughout history God has been saving his people. God has chosen a variety of ways in order to acquire a people for himself: liberation from slavery, deliverance from captivity, and salvation from peril.

The sentence above echoes the opening line of the Letter to the Hebrews: *In times past, God spoke in partial and various ways to our ancestors through the prophets; in these last days, he spoke to us through a son, whom he made heir of all things and through whom he created the universe, who is the refulgence of his glory, the very imprint of his being, and who sustains all things by his mighty word.* (1:1-3)

The psalmist sings of confidence as he recalls his past experiences of salvation. However, while remembering, he also petitions his Lord to save him again: *Into your hands I commend my spirit;/you will redeem me, O LORD, O faithful God./ In your hands is my destiny; rescue me/from the clutches of my enemies and my persecutors./Let your face shine upon your servant;/ save me in your kindness.* (Psalm 31:6, 16-17)

Another psalmist thanks God for deliverance from death: *I will extol you, O LORD, for you drew me clear/and did not let my enemies rejoice over me.* (Psalm 30:2) During the Easter Vigil other verses of this psalm are used with the response, "I will praise you, Lord, for you have rescued me." (LM #42)

The prophet Isaiah repeatedly refers to God as the savior: *God indeed is my savior; I am confident and unafraid. My strength and my courage is the Lord, and he has been my savior.* (12:2) *Your redeemer is the Holy One of Israel, called God of all the earth.* (54:5)

The author of the Book of Exodus, after describing the march out of Egypt and the miraculous crossing of the Sea of Reeds, declares: *Thus the LORD saved Israel on that day from the power of the Egyptians.* (Exodus 14:30)

The liturgical prayers of the Easter Vigil reinforce the remembrance of the great events of salvation. One prayer declares, "Father, . . . you once saved a single nation from slavery, and now you offer that salvation to all through baptism." (EV #26) Another prayer states, "Lord God, . . . the nation you freed from slavery is a sign of your Christian people." (EV #26)

The present moment is the "fullness of time." In the past God "created all things in wonderful beauty and order," but "how still more wonderful is the new creation by which in the fullness of time you [God] redeemed your

people through the sacrifice of our passover, Jesus Christ
. . ." (EV #24) If "the creation of man [and woman] was a
wonderful work, his [or her] redemption [is] still more
wonderful." (EV #24)

Because people recall the salvation history of the past
and experience themselves as part of the salvation history of
the present while looking forward to the future, ". . . we may
be confident that we shall share his [Christ's] victory over
death and live with him for ever in God." (EV #8) Therefore, "Sound the trumpet of salvation!" (EV #18)

The allusion to Paul's First Letter to the Thessalonians
is clear. *The Lord himself, with a word of command, with the voice
of an archangel and with the trumpet of God, will come down from
heaven, and the dead in Christ will rise first. Then we who are alive,
who are left, will be caught up together with them in the clouds to
meet the Lord in the air. Thus we shall always be with the Lord.*
(4:16-17)

For Reflection

a. In what ways has God saved you in the past? In other
    words, what is your salvation history?
b. How is God's saving presence at work in your life now?

Prayer

God our Father,/you loved the world so much/you gave
your only Son to free us/from the ancient power of sin and
death./Help us who wait for his coming,/and lead us to true
liberty./We ask this through our Lord Jesus Christ, your
Son,/who lives and reigns with you and the Holy Spirit,/one
God, for ever and ever. Amen. (TS, p. 9)

4.   *"Like a lamb led to the slaughter or a sheep before the shearers, he was silent and opened not his mouth."* (Isaiah 53:7)

The death of Jesus, the price of ransom, is often compared to the slaughter of a quiet lamb. The sacrificial lamb is killed without ever making a whimper. The sheep is sheared of its wool, and may oftentimes be hurt or wounded in the process, but its coat is taken away from it without a sound coming from its mouth.

Isaac, the son of Abraham, was redeemed with a ram. *As Abraham looked about, he spied a ram caught by its horns in the thicket. So he went and took the ram and offered it up as a holocaust in place of his son.* (Genesis 22:13) In exchange for the life of his son, Abraham slaughtered, sacrificed, the life of a ram.

On Good Friday the presider holds up the wooden cross and sings, "This is the wood of the cross, on which hung the Savior of the world." (GF #17) The Savior, who is proclaimed at every celebration of the Eucharist to be "the Lamb of God who takes away the sins of the world" (TS, p. 564), was slaughtered. The sign of the silent lamb is the cross. "Each time we offer this memorial sacrifice, the work of our redemption is accomplished." (TS, p. 138)

In today's world of transplant surgery, many people posthumously give away their eyes, hearts, livers, or other inner organs so that others may have life. This is done willingly. In a special way such persons are participating in the work of redemption — their lives are exchanged for the life of another.

For Reflection

a.   Who or what has been exchanged in order that you might have life?

b. What have you sacrificed in order to participate in the redemption of another person?

Prayer

Father,/through the obedience of Jesus,/your servant and your Son,/you raised a fallen world./Free us from sin/and bring us the joy that lasts for ever./We ask this through our Lord Jesus Christ, your Son,/who lives and reigns with you and the Holy Spirit,/one God, for ever and ever. Amen. (TS, p. 236).

5. *"With water the prophets announced a new covenant/ that you [God] would make with man [and woman]."* (EV #45)

Both the prophets Isaiah and Ezekiel announce over and over again the new covenant, which has been established by the redeeming action of Jesus.

Speaking for God, Isaiah declares, *Though the mountains leave their place and the hills be shaken, my love shall never leave you nor my covenant of peace be shaken, says the LORD, who has mercy on you.* (54:10) *I will renew with you the everlasting covenant, the benefits assured to David.* (55:3)

Ezekiel speaks of the new heart that God will give to his people: *I will give you a new heart and place a new spirit within you, taking from your bodies your stony hearts and giving you natural hearts. . . . You shall be my people, and I will be your God.* (36:26, 28)

It is through the waters of baptism that one enters into this covenant relationship. However, it is through the celebration of the Eucharist that a person renews this covenant.

The words of institution found in every Eucharistic Prayer declare that Christ has ransomed us with his blood. "This is the cup of my blood, the blood of the new and everlasting covenant. It will be shed for you and for all so that sins may be forgiven." (TS, p. 545)

It was our infirmities that he bore,/our sufferings that he endured. . . ./He was pierced for our offenses,/crushed for our sins,/upon him was the chastisement that makes us whole,/by his stripes we were healed . . ./If he gives his life as an offering for sin,/ . . . the will of the LORD shall be accomplished through him. (Isaiah 53:4-5, 10)

For Reflection

a. How have you most recently experienced the never-ending love and mercy of God?
b. What kind of new heart have you ever experienced?
c. In what way is God's will accomplished in you?

Prayer

Father of our freedom and salvation,/hear the prayers of those redeemed by your Son's suffering./Through you may we have life;/with you may we have eternal joy./We ask this through our Lord Jesus Christ, your Son,/who lives and reigns with you and the Holy Spirit,/one God, for ever and ever. Amen. (TS, p. 240)

6. *"I will take you away from among the nations, gather you from all the foreign lands, and bring you back to your own land."* (Ezekiel 36:24)

Almost every human person has an innate desire to go

home. Home may be defined as a particular country, state, city, or house on the block. Going home is a desire to know one's roots, to establish where one came from, and to further enhance identity. The prophet Ezekiel records God's promise to his people to bring them home to their own land once their period of exile was completed.

Likewise, the prophet Isaiah declares, *The LORD calls you back,/like a wife forsaken and grieved in spirit,/A wife married in youth and then cast off,/says your God. For a brief moment I abandoned you,/but with great tenderness I will take you back./In an outburst of wrath, for a moment I hid my face from you;/But with enduring love I take pity on you,/says the LORD, your redeemer.* (54:6-8)

The metaphor being employed is that of marriage. God is the husband; the people are his wife. A divorce has taken place. The wife feels like her husband has abandoned her. But the husband declares that he will take her back into his home; he will pity her; he will care for her; he will not hide his face from her ever again.

More often than not in this metaphor, it is not the husband who abandons his wife, but the wife who forsakes her husband. People forget about God; God, however, never ceases to remember his people. He never stops calling them back, redeeming and ransoming them. It is not God who moves away from people; people move away from God.

For Reflection

a. When did you most recently feel abandoned by God? Who moved: you or God?
b. In what way have you most recently been called back by God?

Prayer

Father,/in your plan of salvation/your Son Jesus Christ accepted the cross/and freed us from the power of the enemy./
May we come to share the glory of his resurrection,/for he
lives and reigns with you and the Holy Spirit,/one God, for
ever and ever. Amen. (TS, p. 130)

Chapter Three

THIS PASSOVER MYSTERY

1. *"Father,/you teach us in both the Old and the New Testament/to celebrate this passover mystery."* (EV #30)

In one sentence the whole Bible is brought together. The Old Testament, called so by Christians, is otherwise known as the Hebrew Bible. It is a Jewish book which outlines the activity of God in the lives of people before the coming of Jesus, whom Christians claim to be the promised Messiah.

The New Testament is the record of the activity of Jesus, God incarnate, in the lives of people. This book also includes various ways of understanding Jesus as well as various approaches to preaching and teaching about him.

Both the New Testament and the Old Testament are important for Christians. They see a continuity between God's activity in the past, God's activity in Jesus, and God's continuing activity now. The key word is testament, which means covenant. God is in covenant with his people. The Old Covenant has not been abrogated by the New Covenant. In fact, the New Covenant, established in Jesus, is a branch of the Old Covenant.

Continuity is what is at stake here. Time is artificially divided by people in order to make sense of it. For God there is no time — only eternity. God is eternally involved in the lives of his people no matter whether they be Jewish or Christian.

For Reflection

a. How do you approach the Old Testament? How do you approach the New Testament?
b. How has God been at work in your life in the past? How is God at work in your life now? What continuity do you find?

Prayer

Lord,/by this Easter mystery/prepare us for eternal life./ May our celebration of Christ's death and resurrection/ guide us to salvation./We ask this through our Lord Jesus Christ, your Son,/who lives and reigns with you and the Holy Spirit,/one God, for ever and ever. Amen. (TS, p. 248)

2. *"Lord,/by shedding his blood for us,/your Son, Jesus Christ,/established the paschal mystery." (GF #5)*

Passover and paschal are interchangeable terms. Passover refers to multiple events in the Old Testament. Paschal refers to one event, the death of Jesus, in the New Testament.

In one of the accounts of the passover found in the Old Testament, we find the origin of the word.

The LORD said to Moses and Aaron in the land of Egypt, ". . . Every one of your families must procure for itself a lamb, one

apiece for each household. . . . It shall be slaughtered during the
evening twilight. . . . Take some of its blood and apply it to the two
doorposts and the lintel of every house. It is the Passover of the
LORD. For on this same night I will go through Egypt, striking
down every firstborn of the land, both man and beast. . . . But the
blood will mark the houses where you are. Seeing the blood, I will
pass over you; thus, when I strike the land of Egypt, no destructive
blow will come upon you." (Exodus 12:1, 3, 6-7, 11-13)

A second account of the promulgation of the passover
is found in the same chapter of the Book of Exodus.

Moses called all the elders of Israel and said to them, "Go and
procure lambs for your families, and slaughter them as Passover
victims. Then take a bunch of hyssop, and dipping it in the blood that
is in the basin, sprinkle the lintel and the two doorposts with this
blood. But none of you shall go outdoors until morning. For the
LORD will go by, striking down the Egyptians. Seeing the blood on
the lintel of the two doorposts, the LORD will pass over that door and
not let the destroyer come into your houses to strike you down."
(Exodus 12:21-23)

The first event of the Passover, then, is God's literal
passing over the homes of the Israelites, whose doors have
been smeared with the blood of the passover lamb. However, not only does the Lord pass over the homes of the
Israelites, the people themselves pass over from imminent
death to life. They pass over from slavery to freedom. Passover is a saving and revealing action of God.

For Reflection

a. When did God most recently pass over your life? Explain.
b. What enemy was foiled when God passed over you?
    What slavery were you delivered from?

Prayer

Eternal Father,/you gave us the Easter mystery/as our covenant of reconciliation./May the new birth we celebrate/show its effects in the way we live./We ask this through our Lord Jesus Christ, your Son,/who lives and reigns with you and the Holy Spirit,/one God, for ever and ever. Amen. (TS, p. 216)

3. *"By faith he [Moses] kept the Passover and sprinkled the blood, that the Destroyer of the firstborn might not touch them."* (Hebrews 11:28)

Not only did the destroyer of the firstborn of the Egyptians pass over the homes of the Israelites, but, once Pharaoh ordered Moses and Aaron and the Israelites to depart Egypt, two other "passovers" took place.

The angel of God, who had been leading Israel's camp, now moved and went around behind them. The column of cloud also, leaving the front, took up its place behind them . . . (Exodus 14:19).

The angel of God is another way that the Old Testament authors speak of the presence of God. In this particular instance, God functions as a leader of his people. Likewise, the cloud is a sign of the protective presence of God. The pillar of cloud no longer functions as a leader but as a protector for Israel. Throughout the Old Testament and the New Testament, when the sacred authors want to indicate the protective presence of the divinity, they speak of a cloud.

God, then, as a leader, passes over his people in order to lead them. The cloud passes over to the rear of the camp in order to protect the Israelites; thus, God not only leads, but God also protects his people.

For Reflection

a. What is a sign of God as a leader of your life?
b. What is a sign of God as a protector of your life?

Prayer

Father of love, source of all blessings,/help us to pass from our old life of sin/to the new life of grace./Prepare us for the glory of your kingdom./We ask this through our Lord Jesus Christ, your Son,/who lives and reigns with you and the Holy Spirit,/one God, for ever and ever. Amen. (TS, p. 116)

4. *"This is our passover feast,/when Christ, the true lamb, is slain,/whose blood consecrates the homes of all believers."* (EV #18)

In the Old Testament the blood of the passover lamb saved the Israelites from death. They passed over from death to life. The new passover was established by the death of Jesus. In every celebration of the Eucharist, our passover feast, while the bread is being broken and the wine poured out, the entire congregation joins in singing "Lamb of God, you take away the sins of the world." (TS, p. 563)

Jesus, after shedding his blood on the cross, passed over from death to life. The blood of the lamb of God has saved every person from eternal death. Indeed, every person has passed over from death to life.

John's Gospel in particular makes the connection be-

tween the passover lamb of the Old Testament and Jesus as
the passover lamb of the New Testament. *The soldiers came
and broke the legs of the first and then of the other one who was
crucified with Jesus. But when they came to Jesus and saw that he
was already dead, they did not break his legs, but one soldier thrust
his lance into his side and immediately blood and water flowed out.
For this happened so that the scripture passage might be fulfilled:
"Not a bone of it will be broken." And again another passage says:
"They shall look upon him whom they have pierced."* (John 19:32-
34, 36-37).

Also, the Blessing of Water during the Easter Vigil is a
reminder of this same connection. "Your Son willed that
water and blood should flow from his side as he hung upon
the cross." (EV #42) The Church understands the flow of
water to be the birth of baptism and the shedding of blood to
be the birth of the eucharist. Both baptism and eucharist, as
shall be seen later, are passover events.

In the past, the passover lamb was used yearly to remember the great event of deliverance of the Israelites by
God. Today, water, bread, and wine are used to remember
the great event of deliverance by God in the person of Jesus.

For Reflection

a. Whose blood has saved you from death?
b. From what has God most recently delivered you?

Prayer

Almighty, ever-living God,/you have given the human race
Jesus Christ our Savior/as a model of humility./He fulfilled
your will/by becoming man and giving his life on the cross./
Help us to bear witness to you/by following his example of

suffering/and make us worthy to share in his resurrection./ We ask this through our Lord Jesus Christ, your Son,/who lives and reigns with you and the Holy Spirit,/one God, for ever and ever. Amen. (TS, p. 126)

5. *"Lord,/send down your abundant blessing/upon your people who have devoutly recalled the death of your Son/ in the sure hope of the resurrection."* (GF #28)

More often than not when the Church in the liturgy mentions the death and resurrection of Jesus, the reference is to the paschal mystery. The events of the past are the rich soil out of which grows the concept of the passover or, as it is otherwise referred to, the paschal mystery.

Mystery is not to be understood as that which is incomprehensible. Rather, mystery is the process whereby God reveals himself or lets himself be known by means of various events. In the passover of Israel, the passover of the angel of the Lord, and the passover of the cloud, God revealed himself to his people.

Because there is no time with God, one can say that God is eternally revealing himself to people. The Bible records many of these mysteries, but there are many more that take place daily. Jesus, of course, was the supreme revelation of God, for in Jesus God chose human flesh — like everyone — to be the means of his self-disclosure.

The mystery of God can be found in the ocean, in the mountains, and most importantly in the lives of people. Indeed, every person, because he or she is created in the image and likeness of God, is a mystery — a revelation — of God.

For Reflection

a. In what most recent event from your life do you believe that God revealed himself to you? How did this take place?
b. In what most recent event from the life of your family do you believe that God revealed himself to your family? How did this take place?

Prayer

Father,/help us to be ready to celebrate the great paschal mystery./Make our love grow each day/as we [celebrate] the feast of our salvation./We ask this through our Lord Jesus Christ, your Son,/who lives and reigns with you and the Holy Spirit,/one God, for ever and ever. Amen. (TS, p. 103)

6. *"On this most holy night,/. . . our Lord Jesus Christ passed from death to life. . . ./This is the passover of the Lord . . ."* (EV #8)

The passover mystery or paschal mystery of Jesus is God's revelation of himself in the events of the life of Jesus. There are five such events: suffering, death, resurrection, ascension, and the gift of the Holy Spirit. In each of these events, God was disclosing himself not only to Jesus but to all people.

These great events are recalled and celebrated within the Eucharistic Prayer of every celebration of the Eucharist.

"Father, we celebrate the memory of Christ, your Son. We, your people and your ministers, recall his passion, his resurrection from the dead, and his ascension into glory . . ." (TS, p. 546)

"In memory of his death and resurrection, we offer you, Father, this life-giving bread, this saving cup." (TS, p. 550)

"Father, calling to mind the death your Son endured for our salvation, his glorious resurrection and ascension into heaven, and ready to greet him when he comes again, we offer you in thanksgiving this holy and living sacrifice." (TS, p. 554)

"Father, we now celebrate this memorial of our redemption. We recall Christ's death, his descent among the dead, his resurrection, and his ascension to your right hand . . ." (TS, p. 559)

"We do now what Jesus told us to do. We remember his death and his resurrection . . ." (TS, p. 1105)

"And so, loving Father, we remember that Jesus died and rose again to save the world." (TS, p. 1111)

"God our Father, we remember with joy all that Jesus did to save us. In this holy sacrifice, which he gave us as a gift to his Church, we remember his death and resurrection." (TS, p. 1117)

"We do this in memory of Jesus Christ, our Passover and our lasting peace. We celebrate his death and resurrection . . ." (TS, p. 1126)

"Lord our God, your Son has entrusted to us this pledge of his love. We celebrate the memory of his death and resurrection . . ." (TS, p. 1131)

For Reflection

a. What signs are used in the celebration of the Eucharist to enable the remembering of the past events of God's revelation in his Son?

b. What signs are used in the celebration of the Eucharist to spark the awareness that God is continuing to do great deeds whereby he discloses himself to people?

Prayer

Father,/. . . help us to understand the meaning/of your Son's death and resurrection,/and teach us to reflect it in our lives./Grant this through our Lord Jesus Christ, your Son,/ who lives and reigns with you and the Holy Spirit, one God, for ever and ever. Amen. (TS, p. 82)

7. *"Our paschal lamb, Christ, has been sacrificed."*
   (1 Corinthians 5:7)

During the Easter Season, there are five optional Easter Prefaces to be used with the Eucharistic Prayers in every celebration of the Eucharist. All five prefaces praise the Father "with greater joy than ever" during the Easter Season "when Christ became our paschal sacrifice." (TS, p. 417)

The fifth Easter Preface expands on the sacrifice motif. "As he [Christ] offered his body on the cross, his perfect sacrifice fulfilled all others. As he gave himself into your [the Father's] hands for our salvation, he showed himself to be the priest, the altar, and the lamb of sacrifice." (TS, p. 423)

Christ's sacrifice of his body and blood on the cross is named the perfect sacrifice, which fulfills all those of the Old Testament. This theme is found particularly in the Letter to the Hebrews. *We have been consecrated through the offering of the body of Jesus Christ once for all. Every priest stands daily at his ministry, offering frequently those same sacrifices that can never take away sins. But this one [Jesus] offered one sacrifice for sins, and took his seat forever at the right hand of God . . ."* (Hebrews 10:10-12)

As a priest, Christ gave himself into the hands of the Father for our salvation. *But when Christ came as high priest of the good things that have come to be, passing through the greater and more perfect tabernacle not made by hands, that is, not belonging to this creation, he entered once for all into the sanctuary, not with the blood of goats and calves but with his own blood, thus obtaining eternal redemption.* (Hebrews 9:11-12)

But Christ is not only the priest, he is also the altar, the place of the offering. When a new altar is dedicated, the Prayer of Dedication states that the Father brings "to perfection in Christ the mystery of the one true altar prefigured in . . . many altars of old." (DCA, Chapter IV, #48)

After the great flood, Noah built an altar. Abraham "constructed an altar on which to slay Isaac, his only son." (DCA, Chapter IV, #48) And Moses "built an altar on which was cast the blood of a lamb: so prefiguring the altar of the cross." (DCA, Chapter IV, #48)

The presider prays that the altar will be made "a sign of Christ from whose pierced side flowed blood and water, which ushered in the sacraments of the Church." (DCA, Chapter IV, #48)

Summarizing the priesthood theme and the altar theme, the prayer asks that the altar be made "the center of . . . praise and thanksgiving until we arrive at the eternal tabernacle, where, together with Christ, high priest and living altar, we will offer . . . an everlasting sacrifice of praise." (DCA, Chapter IV, #48)

Many writers in the Church "see in the altar a sign of Christ himself" and affirm that "the altar is Christ" (DCA, Chapter IV, #4) Another section of the Prayer of Dedication mentioned above not only summarizes the Christ-as-priest and the Christ-as-altar themes, but leads into the next aspect, Christ-as-lamb.

"All this Christ has fulfilled in the paschal mystery: as priest and victim he freely mounted the tree of the cross and give himself to you, Father, as the one perfect oblation." (DCA, Chapter IV, #48)

To state that Christ is the perfect oblation is to say that he is the offering. Just as the passover lamb was sacrificed that those who shared in it might pass over from death to life, so Christians share in the passover lamb, Jesus, by eating his body and drinking his blood that they may pass over from death to life. "In his sacrifice the new covenant is sealed." (DCA, Chapter IV, #48)

Christ, then, is the offerer, the place of offering, and the offered. He is the perfect passover, the perfect paschal sacrifice.

For Reflection

a. How do you function as a priest like Christ?
b. How are you an altar like Christ?
c. How are you a lamb of sacrifice like Christ?

Prayer

Father,/for your glory and our salvation/you appointed Jesus Christ eternal High Priest./May the people he gained for you by his blood/come to share in the power of his cross and resurrection/by celebrating his memorial in [the] eucharist,/for he lives and reigns with you and the Holy Spirit,/one God, for ever and ever. Amen. (TS, p. 936)

8. *"God our Father,/we are gathered here to share in the supper/which your only Son left to his Church to reveal his love./He gave it to us when he was about to die/and commanded us to celebrate it as the new and eternal sacrifice."* (TS, p. 136)

The Evening Mass of the Lord's Supper, which begins the Easter Triduum on Holy Thursday, commemorates the institution of the Eucharist. The Opening Prayer of the liturgy, given above, emphasizes four themes of the Eucharistic Celebration.

The Eucharist is, first of all, a supper. Matthew, Mark and Luke locate the last supper of Jesus within the context of the passover meal — the yearly commemoration of the great escape of Israel from Egypt, the pass over from death to life. John does not include a eucharistic institution narrative, but places the death of Jesus on the cross at the same time as the passover lambs would have been slaughtered in the temple. In the Johannine understanding, Jesus is the new passover lamb; he is slaughtered for the sins of the world; he passes over from death to life.

One of the earliest references to the celebration of the Lord's Supper is found in the first letter of Paul to the Corinthians. Paul explains, *I received from the Lord what I also handed on to you, that the Lord Jesus, on the night he was handed over, took bread, and, after he had given thanks, broke it and said, "This is my body that is for you. Do this in remembrance of me." In the same way also the cup, after supper, saying, "This cup is the new covenant of my blood. Do this, as often as you drink it, in remembrance of me." For as often as you eat this bread and drink the cup, you proclaim the death of the Lord until he comes.* (11:23-26)

It is while eating a meal with someone that one gets to know that person. Lunch and dinner (or supper) are prime opportunities for sharing with others. When food is shared, people are shared. When food is shared around, people are being passed around. On special occasions such as Easter, Christmas, weddings, baptisms, and funerals, families gather together and share a meal. They also share each other. A lot is disclosed during a meal. A lot of life is broken and poured out during a meal.

For Reflection

a. What was the most recent meal that you shared with your family?
b. What did you discover about each of the members of your family?

Prayer

Father,/you have brought to fulfillment the work of our redemption/through the Easter mystery of Christ your Son./ May we who faithfully proclaim his death and resurrection in these sacramental signs/experience the constant growth of your salvation in our lives./We ask this through our Lord Jesus Christ, your Son,/who lives and reigns with you and the Holy Spirit,/one God, for ever and ever. Amen. (TS, p. 934)

9. *"As I have loved you, so you also should love one another."* (John 13:34)

The second theme of the Holy Thursday Evening Mass of the Lord's Supper is that the Eucharist reveals Christ's love. This is acted out in the Holy Thursday liturgy by the washing of feet. The narrative of Jesus washing the feet of his disciples is found only in John's Gospel, which has no eucharistic institution narrative.

After washing their feet, Jesus asks the disciples, *Do you realize what I have done for you? You call me "teacher" and "master," and rightly so, for indeed I am. If I, therefore, the master and teacher, have washed your feet, you ought to wash one another's feet. I have given you a model to follow, so that as I have done for you, you should also do.* (John 13:12-15)

After this, the Johannine Jesus makes the announcement of Judas' betrayal, and once Judas has left the gathering, Jesus uses the occasion to teach the disciples. *I give you a new commandment: love one another. As I have loved you, so you also should love one another. This is how all will know that you are my disciples, if you have love for one another.* (John 13:34-35)

The Holy Eucharist II Preface summarizes this theme of love. "In this great sacrament you [Father] feed your people and strengthen them in holiness, so that the family of [humankind] may come to walk in the light of one faith, in one communion of love." (TS, p. 469)

Love is demonstrated by washing feet. This does not have to be taken literally. The person who shares a cup of coffee with another may be washing feet. The visit one makes to another may be the way that person washes another's feet. When parents care enough to discipline their children, they are washing their children's feet. Likewise, when children respect their parents, they wash the feet of their parents. In the course of a day, a lot of feet get washed; the motivation is love.

For Reflection

a. Who has most recently washed your feet? How was this done?

b. Whose feet have you most recently washed? How did you do this?

Prayer

Father,/by the blood of your own Son/you have set all men [and women] free and saved us from death./Continue your work of love within us,/that by constantly celebrating the mystery of our salvation/we may reach the eternal life it promises./We ask this through our Lord Jesus Christ, your Son,/who lives and reigns with you and the Holy Spirit,/one God, for ever and ever. Amen. (TS, p. 938)

10. *"Jesus said, 'I thirst.' There was a vessel filled with common wine. So they put a sponge soaked in wine on a sprig of hyssop and put it up to his mouth. When Jesus had taken the wine, he said, 'It is finished.' And bowing his head, he handed over the spirit."* (John 19:28-30)

The third theme of the Holy Thursday celebration concerns the imminent death of Jesus. The supper is not only a prelude to his death, but it is a celebration of his death. The Eucharist continues to proclaim the death of Jesus, while waiting for his coming again in glory.

The third acclamation following the words of institution in the Eucharistic Prayers best exemplifies this point: "When we eat this bread and drink this cup, we proclaim your death, Lord Jesus, until you come in glory." (TS, p. 545) As has already been seen, one aspect of the paschal mystery is the death of Jesus. "Christ has given us this memorial of his passion to bring us its saving power until the end of time." (TS, p. 469)

Christ has "taught us to make this offering in his memory. As we eat his body which he gave for us, we grow in strength. As we drink his blood which he poured out for us, we are washed clean." (TS, p. 467) "We come then to this wonderful sacrament to be fed at . . . table and grow into the likeness of the risen Christ." (TS, p. 469)

In the renewed understanding of the sacraments of Vatican Council II, the Anointing of the Sick is understood to be for the sick and not for the dying. The sacrament for the dying is the Eucharist. When it is carried to the dying it is called Viaticum, food for the journey. Strength for the passage through death to new life is provided by the Eucharist.

Even now, as the community shares in the passover feast, "we receive new life from the supper [the] Son gave us in this world," and it seeks to "find full contentment in the meal it hopes to share in [the] eternal kingdom." (TS, p. 139) Because each person will one day die, he or she needs food for the journey from life through death to new life.

For Reflection

a. In what ways does the Eucharist strengthen you for your journey through life?
b. In what ways does your life proclaim the death of the Lord until he comes again in glory?

Prayer

Father,/your Son, Jesus Christ, is our way, our truth, and our life./[We entrust ourselves] to you/with full confidence in all your promises./Refresh [us] with the body and blood of your Son/and lead [us] to your kingdom in peace./We ask this through our Lord Jesus Christ, your Son,/who lives and

reigns with you and the Holy Spirit,/one God, for ever and
ever. Amen. (TS, p. 839)

11.   *"Then he took the bread, said the blessing, broke it, and*
      gave it to them, saying, 'This is my body, which will be
      given up for you; do this in memory of me.' And likewise
      the cup after they had eaten, saying, 'This cup is the new
      covenant in my blood, which will be shed for you.' "
      (Luke 22:19-20)

Celebrating the new and eternal sacrifice is the fourth
theme found in the Holy Thursday Evening Mass of the
Lord's Supper. Sacrifice is synonymous with covenant. Only
Luke's Gospel records the words of the institution of the cup
as being a new covenant. *This cup is the new covenant in my*
blood, which will be shed for you. (Luke 22:20) Matthew and
Mark simply refer to the *blood of the covenant.* (Matthew
26:28; Mark 14:24)

Both Matthew and Mark see Jesus as continuing the
previous covenant; Luke, obviously, sees something new
taking place.

The Church has adopted the words of Luke. The institution narrative in all of the Eucharistic Prayers declares
that "this is the cup of my blood, the blood of the new and
everlasting covenant." (TS, p. 545)

The sacrifice aspect of this fourth theme echoes the
priesthood of Christ, which has already been examined. "He
is the true and eternal priest who established this unending
sacrifice." (TS, p. 467)

This fourth theme also echoes the offering theme. "He
offered himself as a victim for our deliverance . . ." (TS, p.
467) "At the last supper, as he sat at table with his apostles,

he offered himself to you [the Father] as the spotless lamb, the acceptable gift that gives you perfect praise." (TS, p. 469)

People enter into covenants quite frequently, although they may not have the depth of that which Jesus established. More often than not, such agreements are referred to as contracts. A covenant, however, is more binding; it requires some sacrifice. Both parties of a covenant agree to sacrifice something in order to share in something else.

A husband and wife enter into a marriage covenant; both give up some of life in order to share in more of each other's life. Two persons enter into a covenant of friendship; both sacrifice some of their time in order to have more time with each other. Even in a legal document, people enter into an agreement which assures all involved that the sacrifice pledged (usually money) will be carried through for the greater benefit of all.

For Reflection

a. What covenant have you most recently made?
b. What sacrifice was involved in your covenant?

Prayer

Lord Jesus Christ,/you gave us the eucharist/as the memorial of your suffering and death./May our worship of this sacrament of your body and blood/help us to experience the salvation you won for us and the peace of the kingdom/ where you live with the Father and the Holy Spirit,/one God, for ever and ever. Amen. (TS, p. 348)

12.   *"This is the night when first you saved our fathers [and mothers]:/you freed the people of Israel from their slavery/and led them dry-shod through the sea."* (EV #18)

The Easter Proclamation collapses the thousands of years from the time of the exodus to the time of the death and resurrection of Jesus into one night. The passover from slavery to freedom by way of the Sea of Reeds is so intimately connected to the passover of Jesus from the slavery of death to the freedom of new life that both passovers are renewed on this, the Easter Vigil, night.

It is important to appreciate the fact that both passovers take place during the night. It is in the midst of darkness that Israel makes its escape. Likewise, during the night, the resurrection takes place. Darkness, which so often is thought of as evil, becomes the cover for the good God to work his passover mystery. The night becomes a vehicle for disclosing the day. It is the "most blessed of all nights" and a "night truly blessed." (EV #18)

The darkness facilitates not only God's wonders, but it also enables many human events to take place. Some of the best sharing between friends takes place during the night. Husband and wife usually make love and create life during the night. Throughout the Bible, God often calls people like Samuel and Joseph during the night. Also, many people find a long-sought answer to a problem during the night.

For Reflection

a. What most recent significant event in your life took place during the night?
b. What is your usual response to the darkness? How might you change it?

Prayer

Father in heaven,/the love of your Son led him to accept the suffering of the cross/that his brothers [and sisters] might glory in new life./Change our selfishness into self-giving./ Help us to embrace the world you have given us,/that we may transform the darkness of its pain/into the life and joy of Easter./Grant this through Christ our Lord. Amen. (TS, p. 114)

13. *"The LORD said to Moses, 'Why are you crying out to me? Tell the Israelites to go forward. And you, lift up your staff and, with hand outstretched over the sea, split the sea in two, that the Israelites may pass through it on dry land.' Then Moses stretched out his hand over the sea, and the LORD swept the sea with a strong east wind throughout the night and so turned it into dry land. When the water was thus divided, the Israelites marched into the midst of the sea on dry land, with the water like a wall to their right and to their left."* (Exodus 14:15-16, 21-22)

In order to accomplish his great deeds, God uses people. God works through people such as Moses. Moses does the work, but God gets all of the credit. And this is the way it should be. The point is that God works his great events through the lives of men and women.

The passover from slavery to freedom through the Sea of Reeds was accomplished by God through Moses. For whatever reason, Moses of all the human beings who have ever lived — except Jesus — was a person through whom God worked his triumph.

Jesus, the incarnate presence of God, represents the epitome of what God can do in the life of a person. He, like Moses, was often reluctant to take the first step of that always most important march of life, but once it was taken there was no turning back.

To be human is to be scared of the water — especially if you cannot swim! To be human is to be scared of getting wet or drowning — dying. Initially, Moses was scared of getting wet in the Sea of Reeds. Likewise, Jesus was scared of getting wet on the cross.

However, both Moses and Jesus took that necessary first step of the march — Moses into the sea, Jesus towards Calvary — and both discovered that the land was dry. Both trusted God. Moses found freedom like a wall to the right and to the left. Jesus found new life beyond description. God led Moses and Jesus through their individual passovers.

Today, God continues to work his great deeds in the lives of people who trust him. Where there seems to be the obstacle of the sea, faith perceives dry ground. Where there once was death, faith sees life.

For Reflection

a. What in your life is wet that needs to be turned dry?
b. What was your most recent experience of God working a great deed in your life?

Prayer

Father,/teach us to live good lives,/encourage us with your support/and bring us to eternal life./We ask this through our Lord Jesus Christ, your Son,/who lives and reigns with you and the Holy Spirit,/one God, for ever and ever. Amen. (TS, p. 94)

14. *"Through the paschal mystery/we have been buried with
     Christ in baptism,/so that we may rise with him to a new
     life."* (EV #46)

Baptism immerses people into the paschal mystery. In
baptism the paschal mystery is first traced in one's life. One
begins the process of suffering, dying, rising, ascending,
and experiencing the Holy Spirit inspiring life in baptism.
What happened to Jesus begins to take place in each person,
and it will continue to take place in every one until all have
suffered and died for the last time and been filled with the
Spirit of eternal life.

To be human is to suffer. No one is immune to suffering; it is part and parcel of the human condition. It is just
that some people — for a variety of reasons — suffer more
than others.

Suffering is usually viewed as negative. Suffering is
avoided by visits to the doctor, drugs, and countless other
ingenious ways. While Christians are not masochists who
actively seek suffering, baptism has immersed them into it.
The paschal mystery declares suffering to be a means
whereby God reveals himself in people's lives.

The question posed by the Marcan Jesus to James and
John, after they request seats on the right and left of Jesus
when he would enter into his glory, is also asked of us: *Can
you drink the cup that I drink or be baptized with the baptism with
which I am baptized?* (Mark 10:38) One who has been baptized
into the paschal mystery should be able to answer with a
resounding "Yes!"

For Reflection

a. What has been your most recent experience of suffering
    wherein the paschal mystery has been traced in your life?

b. What new life was the outcome of your experience of suffering?

Prayer

Father,/may we whom you renew in baptism/bear witness to our faith by the way we live./By the suffering, death, and resurrection of your Son/may we come to eternal joy./We ask this through our Lord Jesus Christ, your Son,/who lives and reigns with you and the Holy Spirit,/one God, for ever and ever. Amen. (TS, p. 241)

15. *"May all who are buried with Christ/in the death of baptism/rise also with him to newness of life."* (EV #42)

The baptismal font is at once a tomb and a womb. The one being baptized is drowned in the watery tomb; he or she dies. Just as Jesus was buried after his death, the person being baptized is buried in the death of baptism.

St. Paul explained this to the Romans. He asked them, *Are you unaware that we who were baptized into Christ Jesus were baptized into his death? We were indeed buried with him through baptism into death, so that, just as Christ was raised from the dead by the glory of the Father, we too might live in newness of life.* (Romans 6:3-4)

However, the font of baptism is also a womb. Sometimes called the womb of the Church, the waters of the font that take life also give life. Once a person is totally immersed and drowned in the waters, he or she rises up to a new life with Christ.

Just as Israel passed over from slavery to freedom through the waters of the Sea of Reeds, and just as Jesus passed over from death to life, so every Christian must enter the font and celebrate passover for the first of many times thereafter.

Most people tend to think that they will die but one time. However, many deaths precede the final one. When a child is brought into the world, the parents sooner or later discover that they will do a lot of dying in the process of raising the child.

When a person gives up what he or she individually wants because it is not in the best interest of the community, that person has died. In the case of a moral dilemma, before a final decision is reached, the one making it will have died at least once, if not a number of times.

All of these deaths were begun in baptism. All of these deaths are passovers, celebrations of the paschal mystery.

For Reflection

a. When have you most recently died?
b. What followed your death experience?

Prayer

God our Father,/by raising Christ your Son/you conquered the power of death/and opened for us the way to eternal life./ Let our celebration . . ./raise us up and renew our lives/by the Spirit that is within us./Grant this through our Lord Jesus Christ, your Son,/who lives and reigns with you and the Holy Spirit,/one God, for ever and ever. Amen. (TS, p. 208)

16.   *"Through water you [God] set your people free,/and
      quenched their thirst in the desert."* (EV #45)

Dying is an experience of freedom. At first it may not
seem like it, but only those who have willingly embraced the
paschal mystery and died know the true freedom that dying
can bring.

One of the blessings for the water during the Holy
Saturday liturgy refers to the crossing of the Sea of Reeds as
an action of setting Israel free. It must be remembered that
the people of Israel were dead in slavery before they were set
free. Likewise, Jesus was dead and buried in the tomb before
he was set free.

Once death is experienced, the freedom that follows it
is also experienced. Only death can quench the thirst that
every person has for this new life. It is similar to one who has
wandered in a desert for a long time and suddenly stumbles
upon a pool of cool water.

Of course, for the Christian this search for death and
freedom begins in baptism, where he or she celebrates the
paschal mystery for the first time. If he or she is true to the
Christian way of life, then life becomes a constant cycle of
death and life.

For Reflection

a.   When did you most recently have your thirst for freedom
     satisfied?
b.   What kind of an experience preceded the slaking of this
     thirst?

Prayer

Father,/your Son came among us as a slave/to free the

human race from the bondage of sin./Rescue those unjustly deprived of liberty/and restore them to the freedom you wish for all men [and women] as your sons [and daughters]./ We ask this through our Lord Jesus Christ, your Son,/who lives and reigns with you and the Holy Spirit,/one God, for ever and ever. Amen. (TS, p. 915)

17. *"[Jesus] raised his hands, and blessed them [the disciples]. As he blessed them he parted from them and was taken up to heaven."* (Luke 24:50-51)

It is possible to say that Jesus was caught up in the paschal mystery. The result of really getting involved in the process of suffering, death, and resurrection leaves a person with a new view of life, people, and things. Such experience teases and expands one's vision of reality.

We need only to ask a person who has contracted a terminal illness. Such a one endures much suffering, repeatedly dies, and continuously discovers new life, and finds that his or her vision of reality is expanded. Life, people, and things are seen through a new pair of glasses.

Some people experience this process while watching a movie or a play. They sympathize with the characters to such a degree that they suffer with them; they die with them; they celebrate newfound life with them; and they leave the movie or play with an expanded vision of life, people, and things.

This new lens that people acquire is the result of their immersion into the paschal mystery in baptism. The more a person lets the mystery work, the greater the vision such an individual acquires. The Christian vision has no limits, because it is grounded in the unlimited God.

For Reflection

a. Because of a suffering, death, and resurrection experience, did you discover that you acquired a new vision of
   any kind? What was this new vision?
b. In what ways has your life been altered because of this
   new vision?

Prayer

Father all-powerful, God of love,/you have raised our Lord
Jesus Christ from death to life,/resplendent in glory as King
of creation./Open our hearts,/free all the world to rejoice in
his peace,/to glory in his justice, to live in his love./Bring all
[humankind] together in Jesus Christ your Son,/whose
kingdom is with you and the Holy Spirit,/one God, for ever
and ever. Amen. (TS, p. 352)

18.   *"If I do not go, the Advocate will not come to you. But if
      I go, I will send him to you."* (John 16:7)

   The paschal mystery is completed with the gift of the
Spirit, who is referred to in John's Gospel as the Advocate or
the Paraclete. The Spirit is the force of the new life and
vision that a Christian experiences as he or she continues to
live the paschal mystery.
   The individual who suffers, dies, rises, and is revisioned
is moved by an unseen strong driving wind to seek out more
experiences of the paschal mystery. Such a person is on fire
with a life that keeps spreading. He or she cannot cease
declaring all that God does in his or her life.
   To get to this point, however, is never an easy task. The

repeated suffering and death that is necessary more often than not causes most people to seek cover. New life is terribly painful for it involves a lot of change. The revisioning that must take place means that one's world is always in a state of flux. Every experience is contemplated, and life is adjusted according to the results. The ridicule that one must endure from others who have never experienced the wide avenues of such paschal mystery existence is itself enough to make one want to be content with boredom.

It is no wonder, then, that few people make it to the point of being filled with the Spirit. However, those who do are easily recognized by the noise they make. Their renewing sense of the presence of God in their lives provides a security that defies the powers of the world.

For Reflection

a. When have you most recently experienced the Holy Spirit?
b. What was the result of this experience of the Holy Spirit?

Prayer

Father of light, from whom every good gift comes,/send your Spirit into our lives/with the power of a mighty wind,/ and by the flame of your wisdom/open the horizons of our minds./Loosen our tongues to sing your praise/in words beyond the power of speech,/for without your Spirit/man [and woman] could never raise his [or her] voice in words of peace/or announce the truth that Jesus is Lord,/who lives and reigns with you and the Holy Spirit,/one God, for ever and ever. Amen. (TS, p. 272)

Chapter Four

A FLAME DIVIDED BUT UNDIMMED

1.   *"This is the night when the pillar of fire/destroyed the darkness of sin."* (EV #18)

The Easter Proclamation declares the night of the Easter Vigil to be the night of the appearance of the pillar of fire, which guided the Israelites during their exodus journey and protected them from the Egyptians. The Book of Exodus records, *The column of cloud . . . , leaving the front [of the camp], took up its place behind them [the Israelites], so that it came between the camp of the Egyptians and that of Israel.* (Exodus 14:19-20)

The pillar of fire is another way of stating that God was guiding and protecting his people. *The LORD preceded them [the Israelites], in the daytime by means of a column of cloud to show them the way, and at night by means of a column of fire to give them light. Thus they could travel both day and night. Neither the column of cloud by day nor the column of fire by night ever left its place in front of the people.* (Exodus 13:21-22)

While the pillar of fire is a saving event for Israel, it is the means of the destruction of the Egyptians. *In the night watch just before dawn the LORD cast through the column of the fiery cloud upon the Egyptian force a glance that threw it into a panic; and he so clogged their chariot wheels that they could hardly drive. With that the Egyptians sounded the retreat before Israel, because the LORD was fighting for them against the Egyptians.* (Exodus 14:24-25)

With the destruction of the Egyptians and the escape of Israel, the sin of slavery was eliminated. *Thus the LORD saved Israel on that day from the power of the Egyptians.* (Exodus 14:30)

Just as God protected, led, and fought for his people in the past, he continues to do the same today. One person may struggle with the darkness of a problem only to discover the answer of light; this individual has found God, the pillar of fire. Another person may face the darkness of illness and discover the light of healing, God. No matter to what it is that people find they are enslaved, the pillar of God's fire protects and leads them.

For Reflection

a. To what have you most recently been a slave?
b. What was the sign of God's presence that enlightened you to seek freedom?
c. In your life what other darknesses of sin need to be dispelled by God's pillar of fire?

Prayer

Father, we are filled with the new light/by the coming of your Word among us./May the light of faith/shine in our words and actions./Grant this through our Lord Jesus Christ, your Son,/who lives and reigns with you and the Holy Spirit,/one God, for ever and ever. Amen. (TS, p. 42)

2. *"Make this new fire holy, and inflame us with new hope./Purify our minds by this Easter celebration/and bring us one day to the feast of eternal light."* (EV #9)

The Easter Vigil begins with the Service of Light, which consists of the Blessing of the Fire and the Lighting of the Paschal Candle. "Insofar as possible, a suitable place should be prepared outside the church for the blessing of the new fire, whose flames should be such that they genuinely dispel the darkness and light up the night." (PCPF #82)

The fire is called new; it represents a new beginning. All of the lights (electric and candle) in the church have been extinguished before the fire is kindled outside. The presider asks the Father to make the new fire holy; he asks that the fire be set aside for a special purpose — as a sign that all "share in the light" of the Father's glory through his Son, "the light of the world." (EV #9)

It is important to note that the flames must be genuine so that they light up the night. The echoes of the passover of Israel during the night as well as the rising of Jesus before the dawn are echoed in this act. It is out of the darkness that God shines.

The same procedure is followed by many people in their own homes during the late fall to eliminate the chill and during the winter to drive away the cold. Hearths have become commonplace in many homes again. Once the fire has been kindled, all gather around the flames to warm themselves. The fire draws people to itself and creates community.

The same phenomenon can be observed on a camping trip. As evening draws near, the first thing everyone does is to gather wood and build a fire. Then, all gather around in a circle with the fire in the center. The fire draws the campers to itself; it joins them together in a different type of unity.

For Reflection

a. When was your most recent experience of being drawn together with others around a fire?
b. How did this experience renew you?

Prayer

God of power and life,/glory of all who believe in you,/fill the world with your splendor/and show the nations the light of your truth./We ask this through our Lord Jesus Christ, your Son,/who lives and reigns with you and the Holy Spirit,/one God, for ever and ever. Amen. (TS, p. 56)

3. *"Faith is the realization of what is hoped for and evidence of things not seen."* (Hebrews 11:1)

The second theme of the blessing of the new fire concerns hope. The presider asks the Father to "inflame us with new hope." (EV #9) This is a prayer that all may be on fire with hope, that all will come alive with hope.

Hope is a difficult word to define because it is so intimately connected with faith. The Easter Vigil fire represents the hope that Christians should have for eternal light and life with God.

The author of the Letter to the Hebrews praises the faith of the men and women of the past. In faith they accepted God's guarantee of the future; in other words, they hoped for the best. Christians have more reason to hope; they have seen God at work in the paschal mystery of Jesus and in the paschal mystery that is traced in their own lives.

In this day and time, there are those persons like

Mother Teresa who in faith hope for the recognition of the human dignity of the poor. There are people like Martin Luther King, Jr., who in faith hoped for the equality of all men and women no matter what the color of their skins. And there are not-so-famous people who every day, by the way they live, radiate hope to all those they meet.

For Reflection

a. Who has most recently been a model of hope for you?
b. How did this person inflame you with new hope?
c. How is hope like a fire?

Prayer

Lord,/fill our hearts with your light./May we always acknowledge Christ as our Savior/and be more faithful to his gospel,/for he lives and reigns with you and the Holy Spirit,/ one God, for ever and ever. Amen. (TS, p. 62)

4. *"So huge a fire was kindled in the furnace that the flames devoured the men who threw Shadrach, Meshach, and Abednego into it. But these three fell, bound, into the midst of the white-hot furnace. They walked about in the flames, singing to God and blessing the LORD."* (Daniel 3:22-24)

Fire has the ability to purify. Precious metals, such as gold and silver, have all their impurities removed by fire. Iron and steel are made stronger by fire. While some think that a forest fire is destructive (and sometimes it can be, if it gets out of hand), for the most part it is necessary to preserve the balance of nature. In other words, a fire in the forest can purify the forest.

During the Easter Vigil the community gathers around the new fire. The presider asks the Father to purify the minds of all present by the Easter celebration. The prayer is that minds will be made pure, that all impurities will be removed, by the celebration of new life. Like a newborn child's mind, which is pure, so Easter, the celebration of new life, has the ability to purify adults' minds.

However, people experience their minds being purified every day. One person may have one usual way of doing the laundry; his or her mind can be purified when someone dares to show him or her another way.

At other times an individual may be burdened with guilt from an event in the past. Simply listening to the other can enable that person's mind to be purified.

In the sacrament of Penance, a mind can be purified. It is healthy for one to confront his or her sinfulness. This confrontation can set the stage for conversion and a new way of life.

Many health-conscious people are turning to daily purification in a sauna or steam room. The fire of the sauna or the steam created from water and fire has a purifying effect on the body. The heat causes all of the pores of the body to open up and discharge the impurities of dust and oil that have accumulated in them. After a few minutes in a sauna or a steam room, a person emerges in a renewed or purified state.

Shadrach, Meshach, and Abednego, the three young men — otherwise known as Hananiah, Mishael, and Azariah — in the Book of Daniel, purified the mind of King Nebuchadnezzar. The three were thrown into the white-hot furnace because of their faith. The fire had no effect on them, but it did change the king.

Nebuchadnezzar exclaimed, "Blessed be the God of Shadrach, Meshach, and Abednego, who sent his angel to deliver the servants that trusted in him; they disobeyed the royal command and yielded their bodies rather than serve or worship any god except their own God. . . . There is no other God who can rescue like this." (Daniel 3:95-96)

For Reflection

a. What has been your most recent experience of having your mind purified?
b. What happened in your life as a result of this purification experience?

Prayer

Lord,/let the light of your glory shine within us,/and lead us through the darkness of this world/to the radiant joy of our eternal home./We ask this through our Lord Jesus Christ, your Son,/who lives and reigns with you and the Holy Spirit,/one God, for ever and ever. Amen. (TS, p. 66)

5. *"God of unchanging power and light,/look with mercy and favor on your entire Church."* (EV #30)

God is light (1 John 1:5) the author of the First Letter of John declares. Because God cannot be seen, the author uses the brightest metaphor that he can imagine — light — in an attempt to describe God. Light is a powerful metaphorical description of God.

It is during the light of day that most people work, garden, play baseball, hike, and shop. When night comes, most people rest. It should be noted that those persons who work during the night usually do so in very bright artificial light atmospheres. Light is associated with all that is positive; night is associated with all that is negative. Light triggers activity; night fosters inactivity.

During the lighting of the new fire of the Easter Vigil, the presider prays that the Father will bring all people "one day to the feast of eternal light." (EV #9) The idea expressed here is one of light that never gives way to darkness — eternal light.

However, this eternal light will be a feast. People will celebrate in the light of God. The building of the new fire during the Easter Vigil is intended to be but a taste of the feast of light to come.

Already people share in the feast of light, not only during the Easter Vigil, but during special occasions in their lives. A family wedding is a feast of light. A baptism is a feast of light. A funeral is a feast of light. In the course of a day a new idea, an insight, or seeing a friend can be a feast of light.

For Reflection

a. When did you most recently share in a feast of light?
b. What do you understand by the statement, "God is light"?

Prayer

Father of light, unchanging God,/. . . you reveal to men [and women] of faith/the resplendent fact of the Word made flesh./Your light is strong,/your love is near;/draw us beyond the limits which this world imposes,/to the life where your Spirit makes all life complete./We ask this through Christ our Lord. Amen. (TS, p. 64)

6. *"May the light of Christ, rising in glory, dispel the darkness of our hearts and minds."* (EV #12)

After the new fire is kindled and blessed, the presider prepares the Easter candle, a single, large wax candle that evokes the truth that Christ is the light of the world. The candle is lit from the new fire, which is holy, inflames with hope, purifies minds, and represents the feast of eternal light. The candle is the means of getting the new fire from outside the church into the church, where it will spread its light.

However, before the candle is lit, the presider prepares it by means of symbolic rites. He "cuts a cross in the wax with a stylus" and "traces the Greek letter alpha above the cross, the letter omega below, and the numerals of the current year between the arms of the cross." (EV #10) While doing this the presider says: "Christ yesterday and today, the beginning and the end, Alpha and Omega; all times belong to him and all the ages; to him be glory and power through every age for ever. Amen." (EV #10)

These phrases are expansions and combinations of verses found in the Book of Revelation and the Book of the Prophet Isaiah. *"I am the Alpha and the Omega,"* says the Lord God, *"the one who is and who was and who is to come, the almighty."* (Revelation 1:8) Similar phrases are also found in Revelation 1:17 and 21:6. *"I am the Alpha and the Omega, the first and the last, the beginning and the end"* (Revelation 22:13) is echoed earlier in Revelation 2:8 and in Isaiah 41:4, 44:6, and 48:12.

Essentially what the phrase tries to connote is that Christ, the risen One, is Lord of all time. He is the first and the last in history. He has existed from the beginning of time with the Father; he continues to be with his people today. *In the beginning was the Word, and the Word was with God, and the Word was God. He was in the beginning with God.* (John 1:1-2)

He is the Alpha, the first letter of the Greek alphabet, that is, the beginning of everything. *All things came to be through him, and without him nothing came to be.* (John 1:3) *He is before all things, and in him all things hold together.* (Colossians 1:17)

He is also the Omega, the last letter of the Greek alphabet, that is, the end of all things. *Then comes the end, when he [Christ] hands over the kingdom to his God and Father.... When everything is subjected to him, then the Son himself will [also] be subjected to the one who subjected everything to him, so that God may be all in all.* (1 Corinthians 15:24, 28)

All time belongs to the risen Christ. He is the center of the universe; everything revolves around him. Even the current system of dating with its B.C. (before Christ) and A.D. (anno Domine, year of the Lord) designations attest to this truth. God the Father has set forth in Christ *a plan for the fullness of times, to sum up all things in Christ, in heaven and on earth.* (Ephesians 1:10)

Therefore, the candle is marked with the cross, the sign of Christ, and the current year to indicate that the dead and Risen One remains the center of time — especially the center of the current year. All life and light come from, revolve around, and return to him. Christ is the center of everything.

For Reflection

a. In what ways is Christ the center of your life?
b. In what ways has the Risen Christ dispelled the darkness of your life?

Prayer

God of love, Father of all,/the darkness that covered the

earth/has given way to the bright dawn of your Word made flesh./Make us a people of this light./Make us faithful to your Word,/that we may bring your life to the waiting world./Grant this through Christ our Lord. Amen. (TS, p. 44)

7. *"[Thomas] said to them [the Twelve], 'Unless I see the mark of the nails in the hands and put my finger into the nailmarks and put my hand into his side, I will not believe.' "* (John 20:25)

After the cross and the numerals of the current year have been traced on the Easter candle, the presider "may insert five grains of incense in the candle . . . in the form of a cross." (EV #11) While he does this, the presider says, "By his holy and glorious wounds may Christ our Lord guard us and keep us. Amen." (EV #11)

By tracing the cross, the sign of death, and inserting the five grains of incense, the sign of fire (light and fire), into the place of the wounds of Christ (head, side, hands, and feet) the Church declares that the One who was crucified has been raised from the dead. In this way, the Easter candle represents the passover of the Lord from death to life. The one who died now lives. It is the same Jesus. Like Thomas, who has great difficulty in believing that the crucified One has been raised from the dead, people can see the hands and touch the side and believe.

The grains of incense are used to mark the wounds because incense is burned on fire. Fire recalls the Holy Spirit, who was sent upon the Church by Christ. Also, the fragrance of the burning incense represents Christ's sacrifice, which was acceptable to the Father. *Christ loved us and handed himself over for us as a sacrificial offering to God for a fragrant aroma.* (Ephesians 5:2)

For Reflection

a. In what ways have the cross and wounds been traced in your life?
b. In what ways is your life a sacrifice, a pleasing fragrance acceptable to God?

Prayer

Father of light,/in you is found no shadow of change/but only the fullness of life and limitless truth./Open our hearts to the voice of your Word/and free us from the original darkness that shadows our vision./Restore our sight that we may look upon your Son/who calls us to repentance and a change of heart,/for he lives and reigns with you for ever and ever. Amen. (TS, p. 90)

8. *"Accept this Easter candle,/a flame divided but undimmed,/a pillar of fire that glows to the honor of God."* (EV #18)

Once the Easter candle has been marked with the signs of Christ, it is lit from the new fire. Then, the deacon, carrying it, leads the assembly into the darkened church. Three times the candle is declared to be "Christ our light" (EV #14), after which "the light from the paschal candle should be gradually passed to the candles which it is fitting that all present should hold in their hands. . . ." (PCPF #83) In this way the flame is divided but undimmed. In fact, the more it is divided, the brighter becomes the darkness.

This is true of all life. The more that life is shared, the more there is of it to share. Person after person has discovered this. Give a little time to another in need and receive more time. Spend a few moments really listening and receive many insightful words. St. Francis said it best: It is in giving that we receive.

This flame divided but undimmed is also the pillar of fire. "The procession by which the people enter the church should be led by the light of the paschal candle alone. Just as the children of Israel were guided at night by a pillar of fire, so similarly Christians follow the risen Christ." (PCPF #83)

"The Passover vigil, in which the Hebrews kept watch for the Lord's Passover, which was to free them from slavery to pharaoh, is an annual commemoration. It prefigured the true Pasch of Christ that was to come, the night that is of true liberation, in which 'destroying the bonds of death, Christ rose as victor from the depths.' " (PCPF #79) Today, God continues to lead his people with his light.

For Reflection

a. In what ways has your life been divided but undimmed?
b. In what ways have you discovered that God leads you?

Prayer

God our Father,/your light of truth/guides us to the way of Christ./May all who follow him/reject what is contrary to the gospel./We ask this through our Lord Jesus Christ, your Son,/who lives and reigns with you and the Holy Spirit,/one God, for ever and ever. Amen. (TS, p. 228)

9.   *"Receive the light of Christ."* (RBC #100)

Besides sharing the flame divided but undimmed during the carrying of the Easter candle into the darkened church, those who attend the Easter Vigil "stand with lighted candles and renew their baptismal profession of faith" (EV #46) after the water is blessed during the third part of the ceremony. Each person holds the fire from the Easter candle as a reminder of his or her passover from death to life in baptism. On the day of baptism every person receives a candle lit from the Easter candle. Just as Christ is the light of the world, so are his followers lights in the world.

On the day of the baptism of their children, parents and godparents were told that "this light is entrusted to you to be kept burning brightly. This child of yours has been enlightened by Christ. He (she) is to walk always as a child of the light. May he (she) keep the flame of faith alive in his (her) heart. When the Lord comes, may he (she) go out to meet him with all the saints in the heavenly kingdom." (RBC #100)

The child is referred to as a light, who is to always walk by the light of Christ. His or her life is to be one spent in vigil, waiting for the Lord to come. Faith is a flame which continues to illuminate the darkness. The Easter Vigil becomes a once-a-year concentration of what one's whole life should consist.

When adults are baptized, their godparents are invited to "come forward to give to the newly baptized the light of Christ." (RCIA #230) Those who are already baptized share the light of their baptism with those who have just been immersed in the paschal mystery. Once again, the Easter Vigil becomes an annual celebration and reminder of what one's whole life should consist — walking as a child of the light, waiting for the Lord to come. "The full meaning of vigil is a waiting for the coming of the Lord." (PCPF #80)

For Reflection

a. In what ways is your life a constant Easter Vigil?
b. In what ways have others shared the flame of faith, the light of Christ, with you?
c. In what ways have you shared the flame of faith, the light of Christ, with others?

Prayer

God our Father,/through Christ your Son/the hope of eternal life dawned on our world./Give to us the light of faith/ that we may always acknowledge him as our Redeemer/and come to the glory of his kingdom,/where he lives and reigns with you and the Holy Spirit,/one God, for ever and ever. Amen. (TS. p. 69)

10. *"Let it [the Easter candle] mingle with the lights of heaven and continue bravely burning to dispel the darkness of this night."* (EV #18)

The light of Christ is so bright that it becomes one with the celestial lights. According to the author of the first story of creation in the Book of Genesis, the first words uttered by God on the first day of work were, *"Let there be light," and there was light. God saw how good the light was. God then separated the light from the darkness. God called the light "day," and the darkness he called "night."* (Genesis 1:3-5)

It was not until the fourth day of work that God said, *"Let there be lights in the dome of the sky, to separate day from night. Let them mark the fixed times, the days and the years, and serve as luminaries in the dome of the sky, to shed light upon the earth." And so it happened: God made the two great lights, the greater one to govern the day, and the lesser one to govern the night; and he made the stars."* (Genesis 1:14-16)

The resurrection of Jesus is seen as another great act of creation of light by God. The resurrection of Jesus is God's new creation. *Whoever is in Christ is a new creation: the old things have passed away; behold, new things have come.* (2 Corinthians 5:17) Christians, then, because they are God's new creation of light through Jesus, are to be lights, as bright as the heavenly luminaries, shedding the light of the risen Christ upon the earth.

For Reflection

a.	In what ways are you a new creation of light?
b.	In what ways do you function as the sun, the moon, or a star and shed light upon the earth?

Prayer

All-powerful Father,/you sent your Son Jesus Christ/to bring the new light of salvation to the world./May he enlighten us with his radiance,/who lives and reigns with you and the Holy Spirit,/one God, for ever and ever. Amen. (TS, p. 60)

11.   *"Who has found the place of wisdom,/who has entered*
      into her treasuries?/He who dismisses the light, and it
      departs,/calls it, and it obeys him trembling;/Before
      whom the stars at their posts shine and rejoice;/When he
      calls them, they answer, 'Here we are!'/shining with joy
      for their Maker." (Baruch 3:15, 33-35)

Like the Easter candle that continues bravely burning,
so is the life of every Christian to continue to shine as bright
as the sun, the moon, and the stars. The depth of the
wisdom concerning light is found by observing the Easter
candle — or, for that matter, any candle.

The candle exists to burn. The purpose of making a
candle is to kindle its wick and let the fire consume it. The
candle is most a candle when it has fulfilled its designated
end — to be all burned up, to go up in smoke.

Likewise, a person who professes to follow the light of
Christ, is one who is willing to be consumed by Christ's light.
Real wisdom is found in fulfilling one's purpose — being so
consumed by the light that death is not a fear. A Christian is
most a Christian when he or she is dying, passing over from
life to death to eternal life and light.

This happens often on a daily basis. A person who is
authentically concerned about another is consumed by his
or her care of the other. When the care has been completed,
the task is finished. Light shines brightest when it is ready to
go out.

One who works for justice is consumed by it. He or she
sees injustice everywhere. By speaking out against injustice,
this individual is consumed by it. He or she breathes it and
lives it. In some cases, the result is death. In others, the result
is silencing. Light shines brightest when it is ready to be put
out.

The words of the prophet Baruch addressed to the

family of Judah are appropriately addressed to everyone. *Turn, O Jacob, and receive her: walk by her light toward splendor.* (Baruch 4:2) Turn, be converted, pass over, everyone, and receive the light of wisdom created by God's resurrection of Jesus from the dead: walk by his light and be his light toward the splendor of new life.

For Reflection

a. When have you recently experienced yourself as being authentically who you really are?
b. When have you been burned up or consumed only to discover that you shone brightest?

Prayer

All-powerful Father,/you have made known the birth of the Savior/by the light of a star./May he continue to guide us with his light,/for he lives and reigns with you and the Holy Spirit,/one God for ever and ever. Amen. (TS, p. 70)

12. *"Jesus spoke . . . , saying, 'I am the light of the world. Whoever follows me will not walk in darkness, but will have the light of life.'"* (John 8:12)

In the Easter Proclamation the deacon sings to the Father asking him to permit the light of the Easter candle to dispel the darkness of the night. The Easter candle represents the risen Christ, the light of the world. Just as the candle fights away the darkness, so did the One whom it represents show people the way, the truth, and the life. *I came into the world as light, so that everyone who believes in me might not remain in darkness.* (John 12:46)

Like Jesus, Christians are called to be dispellers of darkness. This is no easy task when the world more often than not prefers to hide in its darkness. In the midst of the dark mushroom cloud of nuclear weaponry, Christians are to work for the light of peace. When the dark night of family crises strike, Christians dispel the darkness with truth and hope. If power is the darkness that crushes human lives, Christians rush in with the weakness of their belief in the crucified and risen Christ.

Yes, a Christian is one who continues to bravely burn and to dispel the darkness of the night when others are content with extinguishing their lights so that they do not have to see anything and, therefore, they do not have to bear witness to the truth.

For Reflection

a. In what areas of your life do you find that you remain in darkness?
b. In what ways have you most recently dispelled some darkness?

Prayer

All-powerful and unseen God,/the coming of your light into our world/has made the darkness vanish./Teach us to proclaim the birth [death, and resurrection] of your Son Jesus Christ,/who lives and reigns with you and the Holy Spirit,/one God, for ever and ever. Amen. (TS, p. 51)

13.   *"May the Morning Star which never sets find this flame
      still burning:/Christ, that Morning Star, who came
      back from the dead,/and shed his peaceful light on all,/
      . . . who lives and reigns for ever and ever."* (EV #18)

The reference to Christ as the Morning Star is an allu-
sion to the fourth oracle of Balaam in the Book of Numbers.
*A star shall advance from Jacob, and a staff shall rise from Israel.
. . .* (Numbers 24:17) Late Judaism and many of the Fathers
of the Church understood this to be a messianic prophecy.
The star was seen to be Christ. Because it was on the morn-
ing of the third day that Christ was raised from the dead, the
Book of Revelation records, *I am the root and offspring of
David, the bright morning star.* (22:16) The allusion is to the
brightness of the sun, the morning star which never sets.

Elsewhere in the Book of Revelation, the author de-
scribes how the Christian, who perseveres in faith, will share
in Christ's resurrection — his victory over death. This victory is symbolized by the morning star. *To the victor, who keeps
to my ways until the end . . . I will give the morning star.* (Revelation 2:26, 28) The victor will receive the same life that Christ
now shares.

The only other reference to the morning star in the
Bible is found in the Second Letter of Peter. The author
reminds his readers that they *possess the prophetic message that
is altogether reliable.* He urges them *to be attentive to it, as to a
lamp shining in a dark place, until day dawns and the morning star
rises in [their] hearts.* (2 Peter 1:19) The dawning of day is
another way of speaking about the second coming, sometimes referred to as the parousia, of Christ.

It is interesting to note that the Greek word, which is
translated as morning star in English, is phosphoros, which
means lightbearer. Christ is God's bearer of the light of
resurrection, which is given to those who understand the

messianic prophecies, persevere in their faith, and remain faithful to the way of Christ. By doing this, such people are lightbearers — the morning star never sets, and the flame of the light of the Christian continues to burn.

For Reflection

a. In what ways have you been a morning star?
b. In what ways do you already share in the victory of Christ?

Prayer

Father,/you revealed your Son to the nations/by the guidance of a star./Lead us to your glory in heaven/by the light of faith./We ask this through our Lord Jesus Christ, your Son,/ who lives and reigns with you and the Holy Spirit,/one God, for ever and ever. Amen. (TS, p. 64)

14. *"In him all the fullness was pleased to dwell, and through him to reconcile all things for him, making peace by the blood of his cross. . . ."* (Colossians 1:19-20)

It is through Jesus' passover from death to life that peaceful light has been shed upon all. The first streaks of the quiet, peace-filled dawn of a new day offer hope. A person cannot stand before a sunrise and not be filled with the light of hope and over-powered with peace.

This is not the opposite-of-war type of peace. This is an inner stillness, which, even in the face of tumult, retains faith that God will be true to his promises. It is a peace that permits radical faith, trust in God when there is no reason to trust, to have its day. Certainly, this is not the kind of peace that the world offers.

Only the Morning Star, the One who passed over from death to life, can offer this peace. Those who have experienced it hunger for it again. It is found in the gentle breeze while standing alone on a mountain peak. It is touched in the rhythmic lap of the waves on the shore as the ocean smoothes its surface. Peace that comes from God can be found in a friendship which frees and courts a healthy respect for the individuality and independence of the other.

For Reflection

a. When have you recently experienced the peaceful light of Christ?
b. Who has enabled you to trust God even when there is no reason to believe?

Prayer

God, light of all nations,/give us the joy of lasting peace,/ and fill us with your radiance/as you filled the hearts of our fathers [and mothers]./We ask this through our Lord Jesus Christ, your Son,/who lives and reigns with you and the Holy Spirit,/one God, for ever and ever. Amen. (TS, p. 68)

15. *"His dominion is vast/and forever peaceful./From David's throne, and over his kingdom,/which he confirms and sustains/By judgment and justice,/both now and forever."* (Isaiah 9:6)

By his resurrection, Jesus was enthroned by God as king. As the *lion of the tribe of Judah, the root of David* (Revelation 5:5), messianic titles applied to Jesus to signify his victory, Christ is the *Lord of lords and king of kings, and those with him are called, chosen, and faithful.* (Revelation 17:14)

However, Jesus is not an earthly king. He is the harbinger of the kingdom of God. His only ambition is to awaken people to the reality of the presence of the kingdom, which is not of this world. Through his resurrection, Jesus now shares completely in this kingdom; he lives and reigns there and will continue to do so forever.

The light of the Easter candle is a reminder that God's kingdom, which Jesus preached, is attainable only through the paschal mystery. Death is not the end of life and reign, rather it is the passage to eternal life and a reign without end. *The last enemy to be destroyed is death . . .* (1 Corinthians 15:26)

For Reflection

a. In what ways in your life have you experienced God's kingdom?
b. What is your greatest fear concerning death?

Prayer

God our Father,/by your gifts to us on earth/we already share in your life./In all we do,/guide us to the light of your kingdom./Grant this through our Lord Jesus Christ, your Son,/who lives and reigns with you and the Holy Spirit,/one God, for ever and ever. Amen. (TS, p. 97)

Chapter Five

WASHED CLEAN OF SIN

1. *"This is the night when Christians everywhere,/washed clean of sin/and freed from all defilement,/are restored to grace and grow together in holiness."* (EV #18)

The Easter Vigil is the time for baptisms to take place. The third part of the service is "the liturgy of baptism, when new members of the Church are reborn as the day of resurrection approaches." (EV #2) In baptism "Christ's passover and ours is . . . celebrated. This is given full expression in those churches which have a baptismal font and more so when the Christian initiation of adults is held or at least the baptism of infants." (PCPF #88)

This baptismal character of the Easter Vigil is one of initiation; persons are initiated into the community of the Church. Three sacraments form the completion of the initiation process: baptism, confirmation, eucharist. "The elect, receiving pardon for their sins, are admitted into the people of God. They are graced with adoption as children of God and are led by the Holy Spirit into the promised fullness of time begun in Christ and, as they share in the eucharistic sacrifice and meal, even to a foretaste of the kingdom of God." (RCIA #206)

An individual becomes a Christian through the waters

of baptism. "The faith of those to be baptized is not simply the faith of the Church, but the personal faith of each one of them and each one of them is expected to keep it a living faith." (RCIA #211) During the vigil all people are reminded of their baptism, its importance in their lives, and the day that they were plunged into the paschal mystery.

In the quick-paced world of today it is easy to forget the importance of baptism in the life of a Christian. Also, since many people were baptized as infants, they have no recollection other than family stories about this great day of their lives. Therefore, at every Easter Vigil and every celebration of the Eucharist on Easter Sunday every person present has the opportunity to renew his or her baptismal faith and be sprinkled with the water that recalls baptism.

For Reflection

a. In what recent experience has your baptism been recalled and celebrated?
b. In what ways are you living a baptismal life, that is, the paschal mystery?
c. What does your baptism mean to you?
d. In what ways is your faith a living faith?

Prayer

Father,/we need your help./Free us from sin and bring us to life./Support us by your power./Grant this through our Lord Jesus Christ, your Son,/who lives and reigns with you and the Holy Spirit,/one God, for ever and ever. Amen. (TS, p. 7)

2. *"Everywhere throughout the world you [Father] increase your chosen people."* (EV #25)

The Easter Proclamation emphasizes that "this is the night when Christians everywhere" are immersed into the paschal mystery. Everywhere the Church is increased; everywhere people are reborn; everywhere the eternal God is petitioned to glorify his name "by increasing [his] chosen people as [he] promised long ago." (EV #27)

The promise of increase is heard in the Lord's messenger's words to Abraham after he was held back from sacrificing his son, Isaac. *I will bless you abundantly and make your descendants as countless as the stars of the sky and the sands of the seashore; . . . in your descendants all the nations of the earth shall find blessing. . . .* (Genesis 22:17-18) These words are fulfilled in the Church as countless men and women around the world are initiated through the waters of baptism.

The Church prays, "Father, you increase your Church by continuing to call all people to salvation. Listen to our prayers and always watch over those you cleanse in baptism." (EV #29) During the Easter Vigil people everywhere are called to salvation, and, those who have already been called ask God to protect them.

For Reflection

a. In what ways has God blessed you?
b. In what ways has God increased you?
c. In what ways has God protected you?

Prayer

Heavenly Father and God of mercy,/we no longer look for Jesus among the dead,/for he is alive and has become the Lord of life./From the waters of death you raise us with him/

and renew your gift of life within us./Increase in our minds and hearts/the risen life we share with Christ/and help us to grow as your people/toward the fullness of eternal life with you./We ask this through Christ our Lord. Amen. (TS, p. 218)

3.   *"Through the waters of the Red Sea/you [Father] led Israel out of slavery,/to be an image of God's holy people,/ set free from sin by baptism."* (EV #42)

The Israelites marched through the Sea of Reeds and passed over from slavery to freedom. The Church views the exodus not only as a passover event, but the people of the exodus as an image of the Church. Just as Israel was set free from the bondage of slavery, men and women who pass through the sea of baptism are set free from sin; they are washed clean. "The Red Sea is a symbol of . . . baptism." (EV #26)

Image and symbol are two important words. An image represents something else. An image stands in the place of the reality it represents, yet it never fully captures that reality. For example, countless images exist of Mary. Pictures and statues portray the Virgin of Nazareth as black, brown, yellow, and white. The picture or statue represents Mary, yet no picture or statue adequately captures her reality; these artistic portrayals are images.

A symbol is an action; it is not a thing. A symbol consists of participation by people. For example, in eating a meal together, people are involved in the action of sharing — eating and drinking. It is difficult for a person to sit at table and not get involved in some form of eating and drinking because these symbols draw all into participation. In baptism, people participate by initiating — welcoming — a person into the Church.

Today, then, every Christian is an image, a representation of God's holy people. Yet, no one Christian adequately displays in his or her life the full meaning of being set free from sin, washed clean, in baptism. Furthermore, every Christian is drawn into the action of being washed by others and washing others, of marching through the baptismal Red Sea waters as a community.

The promise made by God through the prophet Ezekiel, when the Israelites found themselves enslaved a second time in Babylon, is fulfilled during the Easter Vigil in the initiation of new Christians. *I will sprinkle clean water upon you to cleanse you from all your impurities, and from all your idols I will cleanse you.* (Ezekiel 36:25)

For Reflection

a. In what ways are you an image of God's holy people?
b. In what ways do you participate in the baptismal rebirth of others?

Prayer

Lord,/grant us forgiveness,/and set us free from our enslavement to sin./We ask this through our Lord Jesus Christ, your Son,/who lives and reigns with you and the Holy Spirit,/one God, for ever and ever. Amen. (TS, p. 120)

4. *"Father, look now with love upon your Church,/and unseal for her the fountain of baptism."* (EV #42)

The waters of baptism are referred to as a fountain, an overflowing source of life-giving water, which has the ability to refresh and wash clean. This cleansing aspect of baptism is first found during the Easter Triduum on Holy Thursday. The gospel tells the story of Jesus washing the feet of his disciples.

Jesus *rose from supper and took off his outer garments. He took a towel and tied it around his waist. Then he poured water into a basin and began to wash the disciples' feet and dry them with the towel around his waist.* (John 13:4-5)

One aspect of this cleansing is the destruction of sin. "By water, made holy by Christ in the Jordan, you [Father] made our sinful nature new in the bath that gives rebirth." (EV #45) Baptism cleanses people of sin. *Everyone who believes in him [Jesus] will receive forgiveness of sins through his name.* (Acts 10:43)

It is "God, the all-powerful Father of our Lord Jesus Christ," who "has given us a new birth by water and the Holy Spirit and forgiven all our sins." (EV #46) People are cleansed, forgiven of sin, which is best understood as human failure or fault, the inability to hit the mark, to go aside, transgress, to be unfaithful to the covenant, to separate oneself from the community. Once baptized into the community of believers, a person never has to sin again. However, because of human weakness, people do sin. The renewal of baptism through the Sacrament of Reconciliation restores them to their cleansed, baptismal state.

The prayer of blessing for the water used in baptism declares, "In baptism we use your [the Father's] gift of water, which you have made a rich symbol of the grace you give us in this sacrament." (EV #42) The abundance of water above, on, and below the earth overwhelms sin. By being immersed in water, participating in it, God's grace, his own life, washes clean every person and brings about a rebirth.

The Church prays, "Send your Spirit of adoption on those to be born again in baptism." (EV #41) Just as each person spends the first nine months of his or her life in water in his or her mother's womb, so God adopts people as his sons and daughters by a flood of water of new life. This is why the Church asks God to "bless this water: . . . it refreshes us and makes us clean." (EV #45)

For Reflection

a. In what ways have you been cleansed from sin?
b. In what ways have you been reborn over and over again?

Prayer

God of mercy,/you wash away our sins in water,/you give us new birth in the Spirit,/and redeem us in the blood of Christ./As we celebrate Christ's resurrection/increase our awareness of these blessings,/and renew your gift of life within us./We ask this through our Lord Jesus Christ your Son,/who lives and reigns with you and the Holy Spirit,/one God, for ever and ever. Amen. (TS, p. 218)

5.   *"We know that our old self was crucified with him, so that our sinful body might be done away with, that we might no longer be in slavery to sin."* (Romans 6:6)

The deacon, in singing the Easter Proclamation, declares that on the night of the Easter Vigil "Christians everywhere" are "freed from all defilement." (EV #18) A person who is defiled is desecrated, that is, he or she no longer shines with the brightness of creation, with the light of human dignity. Baptism removes all defilement. The Church prays, "Lord God, the creation of man [and woman] was a wonderful work, his [and her] redemption still more wonderful. May we persevere in right reason against all that entices to sin and so attain to everlasting joy." (EV #24)

Human defilement was removed by Jesus. *Through his suffering, my servant shall justify many, and their guilt he shall bear. And he shall take away the sins of many, and win pardon for their offenses.* (Isaiah 53:11-12) Jesus took guilt and sins and brought these defilements to the cross. Christians share in this freed-from-defilement state through baptism, which is symbolized by "the waters of the great flood" which God "made a sign of the waters of baptism, that make an end of sin and a new beginning of goodness." (EV #42) Consequently, Christians must think of themselves *as [being] dead to sin and living for God in Christ Jesus.* (Romans 6:11) After all, *you have died, and your life is hidden with Christ in God.* (Colossians 3:3)

The prayer that accompanies the clothing with a white garment after baptism captures this dead-to-sin theme in terms of becoming a new creation. The presider declares that the newly baptized has "become a new creation" (RBC #99) and clothed himself/herself in Christ. The white garment is "the outward sign" of "Christian dignity." (RBC #99) The newly baptized is to "bring that dignity unstained into the everlasting life of heaven." (RBC #99; cf. RCIA #229)

God has been re-creating the world since the first day of the initial creation. One of the greater Biblical events of re-creation follows the flood. Speaking through the prophet Isaiah, God declares, *This is for me like the days of*

*Noah,/when I swore that the waters of Noah/should never again
deluge the earth;/So I have sworn not to be angry with you,/or to
rebuke you.* (Isaiah 54:9)

With this confidence, Christians can continuously
approach God and say, *A clean heart create for me, O God,/and
a steadfast spirit renew within me./Cast me not out from your
presence,/and your holy spirit take not from me./Give me back the
joy of your salvation./. . . My sacrifice, O God, is a contrite spirit;/a
heart contrite and humbled, O God, you will not spurn.* (Psalm
51:12-14, 19) God is ready and willing to free all people
from defilement.

For Reflection

a. In what ways have you yourself been freed from post-
    baptismal defilement?
b. In what ways is your life hidden with Christ in God?
c. In what ways do you find human dignity being defiled
    today?
d. In what ways do you experience becoming a new crea-
    tion?

Prayer

Father,/you open the kingdom of heaven/to those born
again by water and the Spirit./Increase your gift of love in
us./May all who have been freed from sins in baptism/
receive all that you have promised./We ask this through
our Lord Jesus Christ, your Son,/who lives and reigns with
you and the Holy Spirit,/one God, for ever and ever.
Amen. (TS, p. 229)

6.   *"Then God said, 'Let us make man [and woman] in our
     image, after our likeness.' God created man [and woman]
     in his image; in the divine image he created him [and her];
     male and female he created them."* (Genesis 1:26-27)

The Easter Proclamation declares that Christians are
restored to grace during the Easter Vigil. Grace is nothing
other than a participation in the life of the Triune God.
Grace is being wise in the things of God, as the prophet
Baruch asks, *Who has found the place of wisdom, who has entered
into her treasuries?* and then answers, *He who established the
earth for all time, and filled it with four-footed beasts* . . . (Baruch
3:15, 32) Grace is sharing in the treasuries of God's wisdom. Confident of this gift, the Church can pray to God,
"Be with us as we recall the wonder of our creation and the
greater wonder of our redemption." (EV #45)

The restoration to grace, redemption, is seen as a new
creation. Through the waters of baptism, Christians are
born again; they are re-created in the originally intended
image of their Maker.

The "almighty and eternal God . . . created all things in
wonderful beauty and order." Christians ask that he help
them "to perceive how still more wonderful is the new
creation. . . ." (EV #24)

Newly created grace is poured out on people in
baptism. They can *confidently approach the throne of grace to
receive mercy and to find grace for timely help.* (Hebrews 4:16)
They believe that the One who created man and woman in
his own likeness will "cleanse him [and her] in a new birth
of innocence by water and the Spirit." (EV #42) So, the
Church petitions the Father, "By the power of the Spirit
give to the water of this font the grace of your Son." (EV
#42)

All those immersed in the waters of the baptismal font

are drowned in grace, and they indicate their response to the Lord's call "by joyfully accepting" his "invitation to the new life of grace." (EV #25) They believe that if they *have died with Christ,* they *shall also live with him.* (Romans 6:8) They have been re-created. Their prayer is this: "May the sanctifying power of grace help us to put on the likeness of our Lord in heaven . . ." (GF #5)

This restoration to a newly created life of grace was accomplished "by the triumphant death and resurrection of Christ." (GF #27) The Church asks God to "continue this healing work" so that all "who participate in this mystery never cease to serve" him. (GF #27) It is in this way that God "bring[s] lasting salvation . . . so that the world may see the fallen lifted up, the old made new, and all things brought to perfection through him who is their origin, our Lord Jesus Christ . . ." (EV #30)

For Reflection

a. In what ways have you been restored to grace?
b. Where do you find traces of the new creation in your life?
c. Where do you find grace present in the world?

Prayer

Father of love,/by the outpouring of your grace/you increase the number of those who believe in you./Watch over your chosen family./Give undying life to all/who have been born again in baptism./Grant this through our Lord Jesus Christ, your Son,/who lives and reigns with you and the Holy Spirit,/one God, for ever and ever. Amen. (TS, p. 217)

7.   *"Thus says the Lord GOD: I will prove the holiness of my
     great name.... Thus the nations shall know that I am the
     LORD, says the Lord GOD, when in their sight I prove
     my holiness through you."* (Ezekiel 36:22-23)

Growing together in holiness is another event accomplished by the Easter Vigil. Holiness is often equated with signs of piety — folded hands, bowed heads, the fingering of rosary beads, etc. Holiness, however, is the degree of a person's relationship with God. Such a relationship cannot be charted on a scale of one to ten, but each person knows deep down within himself or herself what degree of holiness he or she has achieved.

Holiness is not the work of each person — although each individual must invest some time developing it. Holiness is the work of God in each person's life. Through the prophet Ezekiel, God said that he was going to prove holiness to the Israelites, who were in the Babylonian Captivity. In other words, God was going to show his people that they still had a relationship with him, even though they had profaned his name.

In order to do this, God gathered his people from among the nations where they had been scattered, and he brought them back to their own land. He cleansed them of their sin and put his spirit in them so that they could live and observe the terms of the covenant. God told the people that they would be his people and he would be their God.

During the Easter Vigil, Christians pray that "every nation share the faith and privilege of Israel and come to new birth in the Holy Spirit." (EV #26) This is prayer for the gift of holiness, for a strengthening of the relationship between God and his people. In baptism this relationship with God is begun, but it must be fostered throughout life.

People know that they can grow together in holiness

only if God helps them to be his faithful people, "for it is by [his] inspiration alone that [they] can grow in goodness." (EV #28) "Full contentment," the highest degree of holiness, will be had only in the "eternal kingdom." (TS, p. 139) Meanwhile, Christians declare, "Athirst is my soul for God, the living God." (Psalm 42:3) In other words, Christians are thirsty for a deepening relationship, holiness, with God.

For Reflection

a. What is the degree of your relationship with God, that is, your holiness?
b. In what ways do you continue to grow together in holiness with others?

Prayer

Father,/you gather the nations to praise your name./May all who are reborn in baptism/be one in faith and love./Grant this through our Lord Jesus Christ, your Son,/who lives and reigns with you and the Holy Spirit,/one God, for ever and ever. Amen. (TS, p. 215)

8. *"I will put my spirit within you and make you live by my statutes, careful to observe my decrees."* (Ezekiel 36:27)

When adults are baptized, unless some serious reason stands in the way, they are to be confirmed immediately. "The conjunction of the two celebrations signifies the unity of the paschal mystery, the close link between the mission of the Son and the outpouring of the Holy Spirit, and the connection between the two sacraments through which the

Son and the Holy Spirit come with the Father to those who are baptized." (RCIA #215)

Not only is the Holy Spirit connected to baptism through confirmation, but in the Easter Vigil the Spirit is found in the first reading forming the liturgy of the word, "when the Church meditates on all the wonderful things God has done for his people from the beginning." (EV #2) *In the beginning, when God created the heavens and the earth, the earth was a formless wasteland, and darkness covered the abyss, while a mighty wind swept over the waters.* (Genesis 1:1-2)

Some translations identify the mighty wind as the spirit of God, as does the Blessing of Water, which states, "At the very dawn of creation your [the Father's] Spirit breathed on the waters, making them the wellspring of all holiness." (EV #42)

Likewise, when the gospel writers record the instance of Jesus' baptism, the Spirit of God is present. The Spirit had brought order out of chaos at the beginning of creation. Now, at the beginning of the new creation, the Spirit is present again bringing ordered redemption out of chaotic sin. "In the waters of the Jordan your [the Father's] Son was baptized by John and anointed with the Spirit." (EV #42)

All . . . who are thirsty are invited to *come to the water.* (Isaiah 55:1) The Church petitions the Father with the Son "to send the Holy Spirit upon the water of this font." (EV #42) Therefore, those who are immersed in the water will be baptized in water and the Spirit.

The Church also asks, "Lord, send out your Spirit, and renew the face of the earth." (LM #42) All pray that the Lord will renew them and keep them "faithful to the Spirit [they] have all received." (EV #45) "Fill us with your Spirit and make us one in peace and love" (EV #55), the presider voices for the community.

The culminating prayer of the petition for the gift of

the Spirit is prayed over the newly baptized as they are confirmed: "All-powerful God, Father of our Lord Jesus Christ, by water and the Holy Spirit you freed your sons and daughters from sin and gave them new life. Send your Holy Spirit upon them to be their helper and guide. Give them the spirit of wisdom and understanding, the spirit of right judgment and courage, the spirit of knowledge and reverence. Fill them with the spirit of wonder and awe in your presence." (RCIA #234)

It is the Holy Spirit, who, while breathing new life into the whole world, enables every person to *Seek the LORD while he may be found,* and to *call him while he is near.* (Isaiah 55:6)

The preface of the Eucharistic Prayer for Pentecost, the culmination of the Easter Season, states that the Father "sent the Holy Spirit on those marked out to be [his] children by sharing the life of [his] only Son, and so . . . brought the paschal mystery to its completion." (TS, p. 429) It is through the waters of baptism and the anointed sealing with the gift of the Holy Spirit that Christians are joined to the passover of Christ and carefully follow his ways.

For Reflection

a. In what ways has the Spirit of God renewed or re-created you?
b. In what ways has the Spirit enabled you to find God?
c. In what ways does the paschal mystery reach completion in your life?

Prayer

Almighty, eternal God,/when the Spirit descended upon Jesus/at his baptism in the Jordan,/you revealed him as your own beloved Son./Keep us, your children born of water and the Spirit,/faithful to our calling./We ask this through our Lord Jesus Christ, your Son,/who lives and reigns with you and the Holy Spirit,/one God, for ever and ever. Amen. (TS, p. 72)

Chapter Six

HOW BOUNDLESS
YOUR MERCIFUL LOVE

1. *"Give thanks to the LORD, for he is good,/for his mercy endures forever./Let the house of Israel say,/'His mercy endures forever.'"* (Psalm 118:1-2)

Throughout the Bible God is praised for the mercy that he shows to his people. Mercy is kindness toward the helpless. Mercy is God's kindness toward his helpless people. Through the prophet Isaiah, God promises, *My love shall never leave you/nor my covenant of peace be shaken,/says the LORD, who has mercy on you.* (Isaiah 54:10)

Those who sin need only *turn to the LORD for mercy; to our God, who is generous in forgiving.* (Isaiah 55:7) All people, God's special creation, need only turn to him and receive his ready-to-give kindness.

Throughout the Easter Vigil the Church petitions the Lord for mercy. After the initial proclamation of the resurrection, the deacon asks all present to join him "in asking God for mercy. . . ." (EV #18) Again, the presider asks God to "look with mercy and favor on [the] entire Church." (EV #30)

Because people stand before God in all their weakness and unworthiness and depend on his eternal mercy, the

Church prays, "Help us to understand your great love for us. May the goodness you now show us confirm our hope in your future mercy." (EV #30) The mercy that God bestows upon his people is beyond understanding; it makes little or no sense to human logic. In fact, the experience of God's mercy now leads his people to hope that he will continue such kindness in the future.

"How boundless your merciful love!" (EV #18), the deacon sings. There are no boundaries, there are no limits, to the kindness that God shows to his people. God brings them to birth; through his providence he rules their lives; by his command he frees them from sin; and through the saving death of his Son he raises them "to the glory of the resurrection." (TS, p. 533)

For Reflection

a. In what ways have you experienced God's mercy?
b. In what ways do you praise God for the mercy that he shows you?

Prayer

Lord,/guide us in your gentle mercy,/for left to ourselves we cannot do your will./Grant this through our Lord Jesus Christ, your Son,/who lives and reigns with you and the Holy Spirit,/one God, for ever and ever. Amen. (TS, p. 113)

2.   *"Father, how wonderful your care for us!"* (EV #18)

Closely connected to God's mercy is God's care. People are the subject of God's concern. God takes responsibility for his people. His care is wonderful and beyond human capacity to understand, as he declares through the prophet Isaiah, *My thoughts are not your thoughts,/nor are your ways my ways, says the LORD./As high as the heavens are above the earth,/so high are my ways above your ways/and my thoughts above your thoughts.* (Isaiah 55:8-9)

During the Liturgy of Baptism of the Easter Vigil, the presider invites the assembly to help with their prayers those candidates who are ready to approach the waters of rebirth and to "ask God . . . to support them with his mercy and love." (EV #38) The words of the prophet Ezekiel echo here: *You shall be my people, and I will be your God.* (Ezekiel 36:28) Through the death-defying waters of baptism, God claims people as his own. Certainly, this is enough to demonstrate his care.

However, God's wonderful care is experienced every day. To awaken from the sleep of death of the night before to the promise of a fresh new day of life is to experience the care of God. A person who can stop at midday and already see much work done, new ideas begun, or plans for the future in place is one who is the subject of God's concern. In the evening God's care is wrapped around people as they sit at table together, share the highs and lows of their day, and prepare for the night of secure rest. In these and in so many other ways God displays his wonderful care for all.

For Reflection

a. In what ways have you recently experienced God's care?
b. In what ways have you praised God for his wonderful care for you?

Prayer

Lord,/watch over your Church,/and guide it with your unfailing love./Protect us from what could harm us/and lead us to what will save us./Help us always,/for without you we are bound to fail./Grant this through our Lord Jesus Christ, your Son,/who lives and reigns with you and the Holy Spirit,/one God, for ever and ever. Amen. (TS, p. 93)

Chapter Seven

PERFECTION

"Just as from the heavens/the rain and snow come down/And do not return there/till they have watered the earth,/making it fertile and fruitful,/Giving seed to him who sows/and bread to him who eats,/So shall my word be that goes forth from my mouth;/It shall not return to me void,/but shall do my will,/achieving the end for which I sent it." (Isaiah 55:10-11)

Perfection is a quality attributed to God and striven after by human beings. To be perfect is to be flawless, to be complete. Only God can be without flaws; only God can be complete. Yet, that inner, deep-down desire that each person has for completeness is nothing other than a will, which comes from God, to be perfect like God. Here, of course, human weakness gets in the way.

God, however, wills that his people reach perfection. As the prophet Isaiah announced, God's word does not return to him without effect. Just as the rain and the snow effect the fertility of the earth, so God's word causes the fruitfulness of perfection to blossom in his people. God works in the human weakness of his people to bring them to perfection.

In the introduction to the Liturgy of the Word of the Easter Vigil, the presider states, "Through this Easter celebration, may God bring to perfection the saving work he has begun in us." (EV #22) Bringing people to completion is God's ongoing work. It is not a one-time-only event, but a lifetime of recognizing the step-by-step process of perfection. The Church prays that with God's help "may this Easter mystery of our redemption bring to perfection the saving work you have begun in us." (EV #52)

People contribute to this process through their cooperation with God. This cooperation is called ministry. It is service given by people to other people to aid them in the process of completion. After the singing of the Litany of Saints during the Easter Vigil, the Church prays to the "almighty and eternal God" that "the work of [her] humble ministry be brought to perfection by [his] mighty power." (EV #41) People cooperate with God by doing God's will, achieving the end for which he sends his word of completion.

While perfection cannot be totally had in this life, people can and do taste it every day. After a person has struggled with a new direction in his or her life and reached a peaceful decision, a short, fleeting moment of completion is tasted before the next step must be taken. To experience the human body in a moment of fitness — such as walking, running, or other exercise — with all of its parts working together is to taste a moment of flawlessness. Even standing at the grave and declaring the beauty of another's life is a declaration and foretaste of the completion that awaits all people through the paschal mystery.

Christians declare, *I shall not die, but live, and declare the works of the LORD*. (Psalm 118:17) Those who are plunged into the paschal mystery do not die; they pass over death to eternal life. And in that indescribable state which awaits everyone after death, they declare how God was at work in their lives guiding each of their steps to perfection.

For Reflection

a. What has been your most recent experience of tasting perfection?
b. How has the word of God effected God's will in your life?
c. In what ministry are you involved?

Prayer

Merciful Father,/fill our hearts with your love/and keep us faithful to the gospel of Christ./Give us the grace to rise above our human weakness./Grant this through our Lord Jesus Christ, your Son,/who lives and reigns with you and the Holy Spirit,/one God, for ever and ever. Amen. (TS, p. 104)

Chapter Eight

GO!

"After his resurrection he [Jesus] told his disciples:/'Go out and teach all nations,/baptizing them in the name of the Father/and of the Son and of the Holy Spirit.'" (EV #42)

During the Easter Vigil, throughout the Easter Octave, and on Pentecost Sunday every celebration of the Eucharist concludes with the assembly's response of "Thanks be to God, alleluia, alleluia" to one of the following dismissals issued by the deacon: "Go in the peace of Christ, alleluia, alleluia." "The Mass is ended, go in peace, alleluia, alleluia." "Go in peace to love and serve the Lord, alleluia, alleluia." (EV #56; TS, pp. 211, 273)

In all three options for the dismissal there exists one important word: Go! The assembly is sent on mission to share the good news of Christ's passover from death to life and of their own passovers from death to life. The alleluias added to the dismissals and the response indicate that the assembly goes filled with praise for the Lord for all that he has done.

"Let this place resound with joy, echoing the mighty song of all God's people" (EV #18), declares the deacon in the Easter Proclamation. The echo of the mighty song is found in the response to the reading of the crossing of the

Sea of Reeds narrative: *I will sing to the LORD, for he is gloriously triumphant; horse and chariot he has cast into the sea.* (Exodus 15:1) The joy is found in Isaiah's words, *With joy you will draw water at the fountain of salvation, and say on that day: Give thanks to the LORD, acclaim his name; among the nations make known his deeds, proclaim how exalted is his name. Sing praise to the LORD for his glorious achievement; let this be known throughout all the earth.* (Isaiah 12:3-5)

Even in the blessing of water, the presider asks the Lord God to "let us share the joys of our brothers [and sisters] who are baptized this Easter." (EV #45) The good news that is to be shared is filled with joy. The assembly, after keeping the Easter Triduum, is commanded to go and proclaim all of the good news to others, so that they too might resound with joy and echo the mighty song of all God's people.

For Reflection

a. In what ways do you share your passover joy with others?
b. In what ways do you resound with joy and echo the mighty song of all God's people?

Prayer

Lord,/you call us to your service/and continue your saving work among us./May your love never abandon us./We ask this through our Lord Jesus Christ, your Son,/who lives and reigns with you and the Holy Spirit,/one God, for ever and ever. Amen. (TS, p. 101)

Chapter Nine

GROUP EXERCISES

1. *On This Most Holy Night*
   (from a sermon by St. Maximus of Turin)

   "Christ is risen! He has burst open the gates of hell and let the dead go free; he has renewed the earth through the members of his Church now born again in baptism, and has made it blossom afresh with men [and women] brought back to life. His Holy Spirit has unlocked the doors of heaven, which stand wide open to receive those who rise up from the earth. Because of Christ's resurrection the thief ascends to paradise, the bodies of the blessed enter the holy city, and the dead are restored to the company of the living. There is an upward movement in the whole of creation, each element raising itself to something higher. We see hell restoring its victims to the upper regions, earth sending its buried dead to heaven, and heaven presenting the new arrivals to the Lord. In one and the same movement, our Savior's passion raises men [and women] from the depths, lifts them up from the earth, and sets them in the heights.

   "Christ is risen. His rising brings life to the dead, forgiveness to sinners, and glory to the saints. And so David the prophet summons all creation to join in celebrating the Easter festival: *Rejoice and be glad*, he cries, *on this day which the Lord has made*.

"The light of Christ is an endless day that knows no night. Christ is this day, says the Apostle; such is the meaning of his words: *Night is almost over; day is at hand.* He tells us that night is almost over, not that it is about to fall. By this we are meant to understand that the coming of Christ's light puts Satan's darkness to flight, leaving no place for any shadow of sin. His everlasting radiance dispels the dark clouds of the past and checks the hidden growth of vice. The Son is that day to whom the day, which is the Father, communicates the mystery of his divinity. He is the day who says through the mouth of Solomon: *I have caused an unfailing light to rise in heaven.* And as in heaven no night can follow day, so no sin can overshadow the justice of Christ. The celestial day is perpetually bright and shining with brilliant light; clouds can never darken its skies. In the same way, the light of Christ is eternally glowing with luminous radiance and can never be extinguished by the darkness of sin. This is why John the evangelist says: *The light shines in the darkness, and the darkness has never been able to overpower it.*

"And so, my brothers [and sisters], each of us ought surely to rejoice on this holy day. Let no one, conscious of his [or her] sinfulness, withdraw from our common celebration, nor let anyone be kept away from our public prayer by the burden of his [or her] guilt. Sinner he [or she] may indeed be, but he [or she] must not despair of pardon on this day which is so highly privileged; for if a thief could receive the grace of paradise, how could a Christian be refused forgiveness?" (LH, pp. 815-817)

For Discussion

a. How does Christ renew the earth through the Church?
b. How do you experience an "upward movement" in creation?

c. How does Christ's resurrection bring life to the dead, forgiveness to sinners, and glory to the saints?
d. In what ways is Christ the light of endless day?
e. What value is placed on the gathering of the community "on this holy day"?

Prayer

Father in heaven,/the light of Jesus/has scattered the darkness of hatred and sin./Called to that light/we ask for your guidance./Form our lives in your truth, our hearts in your love./We ask this through Christ our Lord. Amen. (TS, p. 300)

2. *Christ Has Ransomed Us With His Blood*
   (from an ancient Easter homily formerly
   attributed to St. John Chrysostom)

"The Passover we celebrate brings salvation to the whole human race beginning with the first man [and woman], who together with all others is saved and given life.

"In an imperfect and transitory way, the types and images of the past prefigured the perfect and eternal reality which has now been revealed. The presence of what is represented makes the symbol obsolete: when the king appears in person no one pays reverence to his statue.

"How far the symbol falls short of the reality is seen from the fact that the symbolic Passover celebrated the brief life of the firstborn of the Jews, whereas the real Passover celebrates the eternal life of all [human]kind. It is a small gain to escape death for a short time, only to die soon afterward; it is a very different thing to escape death altogether as we do through the sacrifice of Christ, our Pass-over.

"Correctly understood, its very name shows why this is our greatest feast. It is called the Passover because, when he was striking down the firstborn, the destroying angel passed over the houses of the Hebrews, but it is even more true to say that he passes over us, for he does so once for all when we are raised up by Christ to eternal life.

"If we think only of the true Passover and ask why it is that the time of the Passover and the salvation of the first-born is taken to be the beginning of the year, the answer must surely be that the sacrifice of the true Passover is for us the beginning of eternal life. Because it revolves in cycles and never comes to an end, the year is a symbol of eternity.

"Christ, the sacrifice that was offered for us, is the father of the world to come. He puts an end to our former life, and through the regenerating waters of baptism in which we imitate his death and resurrection, he gives us the beginning of a new life. The knowledge that Christ is the Passover lamb who was sacrificed for us should make us regard the moment of his immolation as the beginning of our own lives. As far as we are concerned, Christ's immola-tion on our behalf takes place when we become aware of this grace and understand the life conferred on us by this sac-rifice. Having once understood it, we should enter upon this new life with all eagerness and never return to the old one, which is now at an end. As Scripture says: *We have died to sin — how then can we continue to live in it?*" (LH, pp. 644-645)

For Discussion

a. What are some of the "types and images" of the past which prefigure the Passover?
b. How is death escaped altogether?

c. How did Passover get its name?
d. In what way is Passover the beginning of the year?
e. In what ways is Christ a Passover lamb?

Prayer

Eternal Father,/reaching from end to end of the universe,/ and ordering all things with your mighty arm:/for you, time is the unfolding of truth that already is,/the unveiling of beauty that is yet to be./Your Son has saved us in history/by rising from the dead,/so that transcending time he might free us from death./May his presence among us/lead to the vision of unlimited truth/and unfold the beauty of your love./We ask this in the name of Jesus the Lord. Amen. (TS, p. 262)

3. *This Passover Mystery*
   (from an Easter homily by Melito of Sardis)

"We should understand, beloved, that the paschal mystery is at once old and new, transitory and eternal, corruptible and incorruptible, mortal and immortal. In terms of the Law it is old, in terms of the Word it is new. In its figure it is passing, in its grace it is eternal. It is corruptible in the sacrifice of the lamb, incorruptible in the eternal life of the Lord. It is mortal in his burial in the earth, immortal in his resurrection from the dead.

"The Law indeed is old, but the Word is new. The type is transitory, but grace is eternal. The lamb was corruptible, but the Lord is incorruptible. He was slain as a lamb; he rose again as God. *He was led like a sheep to the slaughter*, yet he was not a sheep. He was silent as a lamb, yet he was not a lamb.

The type has passed away; the reality has come. The lamb gives place to God, the sheep gives place to a man, and the man is Christ, who fills the whole of creation. The sacrifice of the lamb, the celebration of the passover, the prescriptions of the Law have been fulfilled in Jesus Christ. Under the old Law, and still more under the new dispensation, everything pointed toward him.

"Both the Law and the Word came forth from Zion and Jerusalem, but now the Law has given place to the Word, the old to the new. The commandment has become grace, the type a reality. The lamb has become a Son, the sheep a man, and man, God.

"The Lord, though he was God, became man. He suffered for the sake of those who suffer, he was bound for those in bonds, condemned for the guilty, buried for those who lie in the grave; but he rose from the dead, and cried aloud: *Who will contend with me? Let him confront me.* I have freed the condemned, brought the dead back to life, raised men from their graves. Who has anything to say against me? I, he said, am the Christ; I have destroyed death, triumphed over the enemy, trampled hell underfoot, bound the strong one, and taken men [and women] up to the heights of heaven: I am the Christ.

"Come, then, all you nations of men [and women], receive forgiveness for the sins that defile you. I am your forgiveness. I am the Passover that brings salvation. I am the lamb who was immolated for you. I am your ransom, your life, your resurrection, your light. I am your salvation and your king. I will bring you to the heights of heaven. With my own right hand I will raise you up, and I will show you the eternal Father." (LH, pp. 554-555)

For Discussion

a.   In what ways is the paschal mystery at once old and new?

b. In what ways is the paschal mystery at once transitory and eternal?

c. In what ways is the paschal mystery at once corruptible and incorruptible?

d. In what ways is the paschal mystery at once mortal and immortal?

e. How is Christ the "Passover that brings salvation"?

Prayer

Father,/may our . . . observance/prepare us to embrace the paschal mystery/and to proclaim your salvation with joyful praise./We ask this through our Lord Jesus Christ, your Son,/who lives and reigns with you and the Holy Spirit,/one God, for ever and ever. Amen. (TS, p. 109)

4. *A Flame Divided But Undimmed*
   (from an Easter homily by an ancient author)

   "St. Paul rejoices in the knowledge that spiritual health has been restored to the human race. *Death entered the world through Adam*, he explains, *but life has been given back to the world through Christ*. Again he says: *The first man, being from the earth, is earthly by nature; the second man is from heaven and is heavenly. As we have borne the image of the earthly man*, the image of human nature grown old in sin, *so let us bear the image of the heavenly man*: human nature raised up, redeemed, restored and purified in Christ. We must hold fast to the salvation we have received. *Christ was the firstfruits*, says the Apostle; he is the source of resurrection and life. *Those who belong to Christ will follow him*. Modeling their lives on his purity, they will be secure in the hope of his resurrection and of enjoying with him the glory promised in heaven. Our Lord himself said so in the gospel: *Whoever follows me will not perish, but will pass from death to life.*

"Thus the passion of our Savior is the salvation of [human]kind. The reason why he desired to die for us was that he wanted us who believe in him to live for ever. In the fullness of time it was his will to become what we are, so that we might inherit the eternity he promised and live with him for ever.

"Here, then, is the grace conferred by these heavenly mysteries, the gift which Easter brings, the most longed-for feast of the year; here are the beginnings of creatures newly formed: children born from the life-giving font of holy Church, born anew with the simplicity of little ones, and crying out with the evidence of a clean conscience. Chaste fathers and inviolate mothers accompany this new family, countless in number, born to new life through faith. As they emerge from the grace-giving womb of the font, a blaze of candles burns brightly beneath the tree of faith. The Easter festival brings the grace of holiness from heaven to men [and women]. Through the repeated celebration of the sacred mysteries they receive the spiritual nourishment of the sacrament. Fostered at the very heart of holy Church, the fellowship of one community worships the one God, adoring the triple name of his essential holiness, and together with the prophet sings the psalm which belongs to this yearly festival: *This is the day the Lord has made; let us rejoice and be glad.* And what is this day? It is the Lord Jesus Christ himself, the author of light, who brings the sunrise and the beginning of life, saying of himself: *I am the light of day; whoever walks in daylight does not stumble.* That is to say, whoever follows Christ in all things will come by this path to the throne of eternal light.

"Such was the prayer Christ made to the Father while

he was still on earth: *Father, I desire that where I am they also may be, those who have come to believe in me; and that as you are in me and I in you, so they may abide in us."* (LH, pp. 582-583)

For Discussion

a. What "spiritual health" has been restored to the human race?
b. What is the "tree of faith" beneath which candles burn?
c. What "spiritual nourishment" comes from the sacraments?
d. How have you experienced Christ as the "author of light"?
e. Today, how do people abide in the Father, the Son, and the Holy Spirit?

Prayer

Father,/let the light of your truth/guide us to your kingdom/ through a world filled with lights contrary to your own./ Christian is the name and the gospel we glory in./May your love make us what you have called us to be./We ask this through Christ our Lord. Amen. (TS, p. 304)

5. *Washed Clean of Sin*
   (from the *Jerusalem Catecheses*, also known as the *Mystagogical Catecheses* of St. Cyril of Jerusalem)

"You were led down to the font of holy baptism just as Christ was taken down from the cross and placed in the tomb which is before your eyes. Each of you was asked, 'Do you believe in the name of the Father, and of the Son, and of the Holy Spirit?' You made the profession of faith that brings salvation, you were plunged into the water, and three times you rose again. This symbolized the three days Christ spent in the tomb.

"As our Savior spent three days and three nights in the depths of the earth, so your first rising from the water represented the first day and your first immersion represented the first night. At night a man [or woman] cannot see, but in the day he [or she] walks in the light. So when you were immersed in the water it was like night for you and you could not see, but when you rose again it was like coming into broad daylight. In the same instant you died and were born again; the saving water was both your tomb and your mother.

"Solomon's phrase in another context is very apposite here. He spoke of *a time to give birth, and a time to die*. For you, however, it was the reverse: a time to die, and a time to be born, although in fact both events took place at the same time and your birth was simultaneous with your death.

"This is something amazing and unheard of! It was not we who actually died, were buried and rose again. We only did these things symbolically, but we have been saved in actual fact. It is Christ who was crucified, who was buried and who rose again, and all this has been attributed to us. We share in his sufferings symbolically and gain salvation in reality. What boundless love for men [and women]! Christ's undefiled hands were pierced by the nails; he suffered the pain. I experience no pain, no anguish, yet by the share that I have in his sufferings he freely grants me salvation.

"Let no one imagine that baptism consists only in the forgiveness of sins and in the grace of adoption. Our baptism is not like the baptism of John, which conferred only the forgiveness of sins. We know perfectly well that baptism, besides washing away our sins and bringing us the gift of the Holy Spirit, is a symbol of the sufferings of Christ. This is why Paul exclaims: *Do you not know that when we were baptized into Christ Jesus we were, by that very action, sharing in his death? By baptism we went with him into the tomb.*" (LH, pp. 596-597)

For Discussion

a. In what ways have you been conformed to Christ?
b. How is baptism a type of death?
c. How is baptism a type of birth?
d. How do people share in the sufferings of Christ?
e. How does baptism forgive sins and offer the grace of adoption?

Prayer

God our Father,/you always work to save us,/and now we rejoice in the great love/you give to your chosen people./ Protect all who are about to become your children,/and continue to bless those who are already baptized./Grant this through our Lord Jesus Christ, your Son,/who lives and reigns with you and the Holy Spirit,/one God, for ever and ever. Amen. (TS, p. 121)

6. *How Boundless Your Merciful Love*
   (from a sermon by St. Peter Chrysologus)

"*I appeal to you by the mercy of God.* This appeal is made by Paul, or rather, it is made by God through Paul, because of God's desire to be loved rather than feared, to be a father rather than a Lord. God appeals to us in his mercy to avoid having to punish us in his severity.

"Listen to the Lord's appeal: In me, I want you to see your own body, your members, your heart, your bones, your blood. You may fear what is divine, but why not love what is human? You may run away from me as the Lord, but why not run to me as your father? Perhaps you are filled with shame for causing my bitter passion. Do not be afraid. This cross inflicts a mortal injury, not on me, but on death. These nails no longer pain me, but only deepen your love for me. I do not cry out because of these wounds, but through them I draw you into my heart. My body was stretched on the cross as a symbol, not of how much I suffered, but of my all-embracing love. I count it no loss to shed my blood: it is the price I have paid for your ransom. Come, then, return to me and learn to know me as your father, who repays good for evil, love for injury, and boundless charity for piercing wounds.

"Listen now to what the Apostle urges us to do. *I appeal to you*, he says, *to present your bodies as a living sacrifice*. By this exhortation of his, Paul has raised all men [and women] to priestly status.

"How marvelous is the priesthood of the Christian, for he [or she] is both the victim that is offered on his [or her] own behalf, and the priest who makes the offering. He [or she] does not need to go beyond himself [or herself] to seek what he [or she] is to immolate to God: with himself [or herself] and in himself [or herself] he [or she] brings the sacrifice he [or she] is to offer God for himself [or herself]. The victim remains and the priest remains, always one and the same. Immolated, the victim still lives: the priest who immolates cannot kill. Truly it is an amazing sacrifice in which a body is offered without being slain and blood is offered without being shed.

"The Apostle says: *I appeal to you by the mercy of God to present your bodies as a living sacrifice*. Brethren, this sacrifice follows the pattern of Christ's sacrifice by which he gave his body as a living immolation for the life of the world. He really made his body a living sacrifice, because, though slain, he continues to live. In such a victim death receives its ransom, but the victim remains alive. Death itself suffers the punishment. This is why death for the martyrs is actually a birth, and their end a beginning. Their execution is the door to life, and those who were thought to have been blotted out from the earth shine brilliantly in heaven.

"Paul says: *I appeal to you by the mercy of God to present your bodies as a sacrifice, living and holy*. The prophet said the same thing: *Sacrifice and offering you did not desire, but you have prepared a body for me*. Each of us is called to be both a sacrifice to God and his priest. Do not forfeit what divine authority confers on you. Put on the garment of holiness, gird yourself with the belt of chastity. Let Christ be your helmet, let the cross on your forehead be your unfailing protection. Your breastplate should be the knowledge of God that he himself has given you. Keep burning continually the sweet-smelling incense of prayer. Take up the sword of the Spirit. Let your heart be an altar. Then, with full confidence in God, present your body for sacrifice. God desires not death, but faith; God thirsts not for blood, but for self-surrender; God is appeased not by slaughter, but by the offering of your free will." (LH, pp. 770-772)

For Discussion

a. How is the cross a symbol of the Lord's "all-embracing love"?
b. How do you experience yourself as a "living sacrifice"?
c. How do you experience yourself as a "priest"?

d. In what ways is death for a martyr "actually a birth"?
e. In what ways can a person's "free will" be offered to God?

Prayer

Father, our source of life,/you know our weakness./May we reach out with joy to grasp your hand/and walk more readily in your ways./We ask this through our Lord Jesus Christ, your Son,/who lives and reigns with you and the Holy Spirit,/one God, for ever and ever. Amen. (TS, p. 112)

7. *Perfection*
    (from the treatise *On the Trinity*, by
    Didymus of Alexandria)

"The Holy Spirit renews us in baptism through his godhead, which he shares with the Father and the Son. Finding us in a state of deformity, the Spirit restores our original beauty and fills us with his grace, leaving no room for anything unworthy of our love. The Spirit frees us from sin and death, and changes us from the earthly men [and women] we were, men [and women] of dust and ashes, into spiritual men [and women], sharers in the divine glory, sons [and daughters] and heirs of God the Father who bear a likeness to the Son and are his co-heirs and brothers [and sisters], destined to reign with him and to share his glory. In place of earth the Spirit reopens heaven to us and gladly admits us into paradise, giving us even now greater honor than the angels, and by the holy waters of baptism extinguishing the unquenchable fires of hell.

"We men [and women] are conceived twice: to the

human body we owe our first conception, to the divine Spirit, our second. John says: *To all who received him, who believed in his name, he gave power to become children of God. These were born not by human generation, not by the desire of the flesh, not by the will of man, but of God.* All who believed in Christ, he says, received power to become children of God, that is, of the Holy Spirit, and to gain kinship with God. To show that their parent was God the Holy Spirit, he adds these words of Christ: *I give you this solemn warning, that without being born of water and the Spirit, no one can enter the kingdom of God.*

"Visibly, through the ministry of priests, the font gives symbolic birth to our visible bodies. Invisibly, through the ministry of angels, the Spirit of God, whom even the mind's eye cannot see, baptizes into himself both our souls and bodies, giving them a new birth.

"Speaking quite literally, and also in harmony with the words *of water and the Spirit,* John the Baptist says of Christ: *He will baptize you with the Holy Spirit and with fire.* Since we are only vessels of clay, we must first be cleansed in water and then hardened by spiritual fire — for *God is a consuming fire.* We need the Holy Spirit to perfect and renew us, for spiritual fire can cleanse us, and spiritual water can recast us as in a furnace and make us into new men [and women]." (LH, pp. 882-883)

For Discussion

a. In what ways does the Spirit change our deformity to our "original beauty"?
b. To whom do you owe your first conception?
c. To whom do you owe your second conception?
d. How have you experienced being baptized "with the Holy Spirit and with fire"?

e. In what ways has your vessel of clay been hardened by "spiritual fire"?

Prayer

Lord,/may everything we do/begin with your inspiration,/ continue with your help,/and reach perfection under your guidance./We ask this through our Lord Jesus Christ, your Son,/who lives and reigns with you and the Holy Spirit,/one God, for ever and ever. Amen. (TS, p. 79)

8. *Go!*
   (from the *Letter to the Corinthians*, by
   St. Clement of Rome)

"Beloved, Jesus Christ is our salvation, he is the high priest through whom we present our offerings and the helper who supports us in our weakness. Through him our gaze penetrates the heights of heaven and we see, as in a mirror, the most holy face of God. Through Christ the eyes of our hearts are opened, and our weak and clouded understanding reaches up toward the light. Through him the Lord God willed that we should taste eternal knowledge, for Christ *is the radiance of God's glory, and as much greater than the angels as the name God has given him is superior to theirs.*

"So then, my brothers [and sisters], let us do battle with all our might under his unerring command. Think of the men serving under our military commanders. How well disciplined they are! How readily and submissively they carry out orders! Not everyone can be a prefect, a tribune, a centurion, or a captain of fifty, but each man in his own rank executes the orders of the emperor and the officers in command. The great cannot exist without those of humble condition, nor can those of humble condition exist without the great. Always it is the harmonious working together of its various parts that insure the well-being of the whole. Take our own body as an example: the head is helpless without the feet; and the feet can do nothing without the head. Even our least important members are useful and necessary to the whole body, and all work together for its well-being in harmonious subordination.

"Let us, then, preserve the unity of the body that we form in Christ Jesus, and let everyone give his [or her] neighbor the deference to which his [or her] particular gifts entitle him [or her]. Let the strong care for the weak and the weak respect the strong. Let the wealthy assist the poor and the poor man [or woman] thank God for giving him [or her] someone to supply his [or her] needs. The wise man [or woman] should show his [or her] wisdom not by eloquence but by good works; the humble man [or woman] should not proclaim his [or her] own humility, but leave others to do so; nor must the man [or woman] who preserves his [or her] chastity ever boast of it, but recognize that the ability to control his [or her] desires has been given him [or her] by another.

"Think, my brothers [and sisters], of how we first came into being, of what we were at the first moment of our existence. Think of the dark tomb out of which our Creator brought us into his world where he had his gifts prepared for us even before we were born. All this we owe to him and for everything we must give him thanks. To him be glory for ever and ever. Amen." (LH, pp. 796-797)

For Discussion

a. In what ways is Christ "our salvation"?

b. How do you experience the whole body of the Church working together in harmony?
c. How does the harmonious working together of the various parts of the body of Christ insure the well-being of the whole body?
d. In what ways do you experience people giving their neighbors deference to the particular gifts entitled to them?
e. What particular gifts do you possess for preserving the unity of the body that we form in Christ Jesus?

Prayer

God our Father,/gifts without measure flow from your goodness/to bring us your peace./Our life is your gift./ Guide our life's journey,/for only your love makes us whole./ Keep us strong in your love./We ask this through Christ our Lord. Amen. (TS, p. 310)